# PORTABLE CHESS COACH

# PORTABLE

# CHESS
# COACH

## JUDEE SHIPMAN

CARDOZA
PUBLISHING

Cardoza Publishing is the foremost gaming publisher in the world, with a library of over 175 up-to-date and easy-to-read books and strategies. These authoritative works are written by the top experts in their fields and with more than 8,500,000 books in print, represent the best-selling and most popular gaming books anywhere.

FIRST EDITION

Copyright © 2006 by Judee Shipman
- All Rights Reserved -

Library of Congress Catalog Card No: 2005937830
ISBN: 1-58042-185-7

Visit our web site—www.cardozapub.com—or write for a full list of books and computer strategies.

**CARDOZA PUBLISHING**
P.O. Box 1500, Cooper Station, New York, NY 10276
Phone (800) 577-WINS
email: cardozapub@aol.com
**www.cardozapub.com**

## About the Author

Judee Shipman, often listed among the top 50 female players in the United States, has been playing tournament chess for over 30 years. She teaches after-school chess workshops throughout the San Francisco Bay area and frequently gives private lessons by phone. Judee currently lives in Contra Costa County with her daughter Clare.

*for Clare*

# CONTENTS

Foreword                                          9

Introduction                                     11

1. Most of the Rules                             12

2. Castling, Draws, and the
   Touch–move Rule                               29

3. Piece Values and The
   En Passant Capture                            39

4. The Language of Chess                         48

5. The Clock                                     58

6. Basic Checkmates                              62

7. Opening Strategy                              75

8. Middle Game Strategy                          85

9. Endgame Strategy                              95

10. The Mighty Pawn                             104

11. Basic Tactics                               114

12. Seeing The Future—
    the Art of Combinations                     124

13. The Ten Most Common
      Beginner's Mistakes                 136

14. Chess Psychology                     141

15. Instructive Games                    146

16. Practice Puzzles                     157

    Glossary of Chess Terms              165

    Acknowledgements                     173

# FOREWORD

## by **Bruce Pandolfini**

Best-selling chess author and subject of the movie
*Searching for Bobby Fischer*

*The Portable Chess Coach* is quite possibly the best contemporary introduction to the game of chess. Based on the scholastic programs of Judee Shipman, this entertaining and insightful volume is the ultimate beginner's instruction book. It contains all the material needed to play chess proficiently and with confidence. Moves, rules, strategies, principles, notation, exercises, tournament preparation, and games are all presented here with an elegant simplicity not found in other chess books. And the glossary of chess terms contains 200 entries! But even more unusual, Ms. Shipman shows a sharp sense of humor and an unusual flair for creative prose rarely seen in the realm of instructional books.

Ideas are explained in the clearest, briefest possible terms, and accompanied by simple diagrams that anyone can follow. Almost every diagram caption provides additional information not included in the text. And topics are often strategically concluded with hints of other topics to be covered in later chapters.

Ms. Shipman frequently provides multiple examples, clearly understanding when the nuances of a concept can become confusing. She remains aware of these potential sources of confusion among beginners, and it's especially in these problem areas that her distinctions are so illuminating. *The Portable Chess Coach* seems to answer questions before they are asked, to address problems before they occur. I've seldom seen so much instructional material so effectively communicated in so few words.

The presentation of the rules is particularly informative and comprehensive—certainly the most concise, yet thorough treatment of them to be found anywhere. This is a vital accomplishment. Chess books written for beginners tend to take too much for granted. Too often, chess writers presume they're dealing with a uniform audience, and a knowledgeable one at that. Ms. Shipman's sensitive text is devoid of all such problems. She is a strong and experienced player, but also a gifted teacher with a keen eye for the mental roadblocks encountered by beginners of all ages. She recognizes that individuals perform at all different skill levels, so she provides a complete treatment of necessary fundamentals, anticipating everything, presuming nothing, and leaving nothing out.

A contemporary classic that makes chess seem easy, *The Portable Chess Coach* might be the first genuinely mainstream treatment of this very technical subject.

I highly recommend this book!

# INTRODUCTION

Chess is easy to learn. So easy, in fact, that this very simple book is ALL you'll need in order to reach a solid, intermediate competitive level.

The *Portable Chess Coach* is somewhat like a human chess coach. It clearly explains basic concepts, tests your understanding with review questions, problems and annotated games, caters to all skill levels, and offers tips on chess psychology. But unlike a human chess coach, the *Portable Chess Coach* is inexpensive, light enough to carry everywhere, and ready when you are.

My father taught me chess before I could read, and chess taught me things that can't be learned from books—focus, concentration, thoroughness, objectivity, and patience, to name just a few. As for winning, let me put it this way...

I once heard a brilliant acting coach say to an actor who was trying his best to stagger drunkenly across the stage, *"A drunk doesn't try to stagger. A drunk tries to walk a straight line."* What, you may wonder, does this have to do with winning a chess game? Nothing. That's the point: Chess players don't try to win. Chess players try to play chess. This concludes your first lesson in chess psychology.

These pages will unleash powers you never knew existed. People will think you're a genius! Read on and discover, once and for all, the infinite simplicity of chess.

# 1. MOST OF THE RULES

A chessboard has 64 squares—32 light squares and 32 dark squares. Vertical columns of squares are called **files**, and are referred to by using the lowercase letters **a** through **h**. Horizontal rows of squares are called **ranks**, and are numbered **1** through **8**. Connected squares of the same color following any straight line are called **diagonals**.

A square is named after the point where its rank and file intersect, with the file (letter) always stated first. In Diagram 1.1, the squares b1, d5, and h6 are marked with stars. This method of naming squares is called **algebraic notation**.

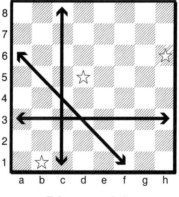

**Diagram 1.1**

The 3rd rank. the c-file. and the f1-a6
diagonal are marked with arrows.

There are six kinds of chess pieces: **kings** (♚♔), **queens** (♛♕), **rooks** (♜♖), **bishops** (♝♗), **knights** (♞♘), and **pawns** (♟♙). They represent soldiers in opposing armies, and each type of soldier moves from one square to another in a different way.

## THE KING

A king moves one square at a time in any direction (forward, backward, left, right, or diagonally). In other words, a king can only move to a square that *touches* the square it's on (except when **castling**, as we'll learn in Chapter 2). The king shown in Diagram 1.2 has eight possible moves (to the squares marked with stars) from its current position on c6. Each player has one king.

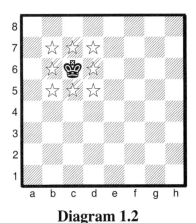

**Diagram 1.2**

**Q:** How many moves would it take for this king to reach f3?
**A:** Three moves (to d5, then e4, then f3).

## THE QUEEN

A queen moves one or more squares along any rank, file, or diagonal, in any direction, unless otherwise restricted. For instance, queens don't jump over other pieces, and you cannot move to a square that is occupied by one of your own pieces. So the queen shown in Diagram 1.3 has 22 squares (marked with stars) to choose from.

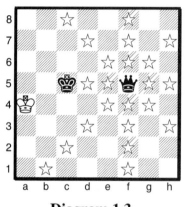

**Diagram 1.3**

The queen is the strongest piece, since it can attack more squares at once than any other piece.

## THE ROOK

A rook moves one or more squares at a time along any rank or file, in any direction, unless otherwise restricted. The rook shown in Diagram 1.4 can move to any square marked with a star. A player starts the game with two rooks (sometimes called castles, but rook is the correct term).

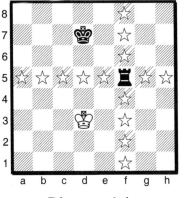

**Diagram 1.4**

An unobstructed rook always has 14 squares to choose from.

# THE BISHOP

A bishop moves one or more squares along any diagonal, in any direction. The bishop in Diagram 1.5 can move to any square marked with a star. Notice that a bishop always stays on squares of the same color. Each player starts the game with two bishops: a light-squared bishop and a dark-squared bishop.

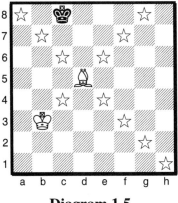

**Diagram 1.5**

Unless placed in the corner, a bishop can attack two diagonals at once.
This bishop attacks the a2-g8 diagonal, and the h1-a8 diagonal.

## THE KNIGHT

A knight moves in an L-shaped pattern made up of four squares (from square of departure to landing square). It travels either two squares left or right, then one square up or down, or two squares up or down, then one square left or right. The knight is the only piece that doesn't move in a straight line, and the only piece able to jump over (without capturing) other pieces in its path. In Diagram 1.6, the knight on e4 can visit any of the eight squares marked with stars. A player begins a game with two knights.

Notice that a knight has fewer moves when placed on the edge of the board than when placed nearer the center. Count the number of squares a knight can visit from an edge (three or four), from a corner (only two), and from nearer the center (eight). How many moves does it take for a knight to go from one edge of the board to the opposite edge? Four. From one corner to the opposite corner? Six. Try it and see.

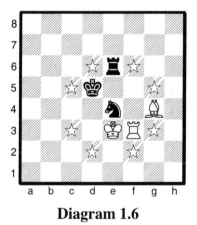

**Diagram 1.6**

A knight moves from a light to a dark square, or vice versa, ignoring any pieces it meets along the way.

**CARDOZA PUBLISHING • JUDEE SHIPMAN**

## THE PAWN

A pawn move depends upon its circumstances (see Diagram 1.7)

1. When moving to an empty square, a pawn moves straight and forward, usually one square at a time. In this example, the pawn on a3 can only move to a4.

2. Any pawn that has not yet moved may advance one or two squares. Here, the pawn on c2, its starting position, can go to either c3 or c4 in a single move.

3. To make a **capture**, a pawn moves one square diagonally forward. Here, if it's White's move, the pawn on e4 may capture the black pawn on d5 (but not the one on e5). If it's Black's move, the pawn on d5 can either capture the pawn on e4, or simply advance to d4.

4. Pawns never move backward or sideways.

5. When a pawn reaches the last rank, it is removed from the board and replaced on the same square with a queen, rook, bishop, or knight of the same color. This counts as one move, and is called **pawn promotion**. Most players promote to a queen, since it's the strongest piece. In fact, pawn promotion is also known as **queening** a pawn. Here, the a3 pawn might promote on a8 in a few more moves, by advancing one square at a time. A pawn may be promoted to any of the pieces just mentioned, regardless of which pieces are still on the board. If you want to promote your pawn to a queen but you don't have an extra one handy, you can:

**a)** Use a queen from another set

**b)** Turn a captured rook upside-down

**c)** Substitute a coin, bottle cap, or any small, weighted object, that will fit on the square, and call it what you wish.

Each player starts with eight pawns. That means it's possible, though unnecessary, for a player to have nine queens.

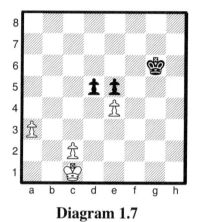

**Diagram 1.7**

White pawns always move toward the 8th rank, while black pawns always move toward the 1st rank.

## THE CHECK

When a king stands on a square to which an enemy piece can move, the king is said to be in **check**. Check simply means that an enemy piece threatens to capture the king. In Diagram 1.8, the white bishop on b3 checks the black king on f7. In other words, the bishop threatens to capture the king, since it can move to f7 on White's next turn.

If you're in check, you must use your move to get out of check. If a player fails to do this, the opponent is not allowed to capture the attacked king. Instead, the illegal move must be taken back, and another move played. A king may not stay in check for even a single move, and may never move into check.

There are three ways to get out of check (refer again to Diagram 1.8)

1. **Move** the king to a square that is not under attack. In this case, the black king can move to e7, g7, e8, or f8.

2. **Capture** the piece that's checking the king. The pawn on a4 can capture the bishop on b3 (probably Black's best move).

3. **Block** the check by moving one of your pieces between your king and the piece that's attacking it. Here, the pawn on c5 could advance to c4, blocking the bishop's attack on the enemy king.

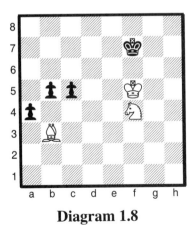

**Diagram 1.8**

A king can never move adjacent to the other king—
it would be putting itself in check.

You have to take your time in order to see every possible check in each position, and to find all possible means of escape. An important chess principle is this one: **always look for checks**. Don't necessarily *play* the check. It might be a glaring blunder. But notice it. Consider it. Even when it looks like a silly move, check is always a **forcing move**. Think about checks throughout the game. The importance of exploring checks cannot be overstated. Use the following three diagrams to practice finding checks.

**Diagram 1.9**

**Q:** Black's knight checks White's king.
Where can White move to get the king out of check?
**A:** White can move the king to either h1 or f1
(g2 is guarded by the black pawn, and h2 by the black knight).

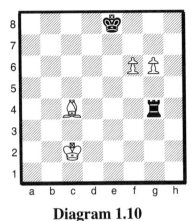

**Diagram 1.10**

**Q:** Where can White move to put the black king in check?
**A:** Pawn to f7, bishop to f7, or bishop to b5.

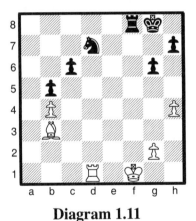

**Diagram 1.11**

**Q:** Is this position possible? Why or why not?
**A:** No, because both kings are in check, meaning
somebody forgot to get OUT of check.

## CHECKMATE

When a king is in check and cannot get out of check, it's **checkmate**, and the game is over. In Diagram 1.12, the white king on b1 is checked by the queen on b2, and has no way out of check. Black's queen and king guard all possible escape squares. The queen is protected by its own king, so it cannot be captured by the enemy king. Checkmate, also known by its nickname,"mate," means that an attacked king cannot escape immediate capture, though the actual capture never takes place. The reason for this is simple: The person who just gave checkmate was the last player to move, so now it's the other player's turn. But the player whose king is checkmated has no legal moves. Since no one can move, the game ends there.

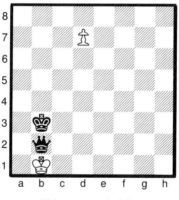

**Diagram 1.12**

Black has just played the queen to b2, checkmating the white king. Game over. Black wins.

Which of the following three diagrams shows a checkmated king?

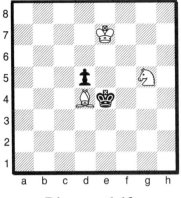

**Diagram 1.13**

It's hard to checkmate a king in the middle of the board because there are so many squares it can flee to. Black's king is checked by the white knight, but can escape to f5, f4, d3, or even d4 (taking the white bishop).

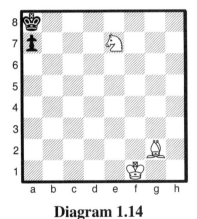

**Diagram 1.14**

White has the advantage, but his knight is misplaced and his king too far away. The enemy king is checked by the bishop on g2, but can move to b8.

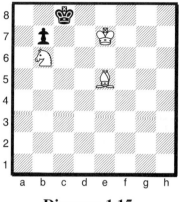

**Diagram 1.15**

A well-coordinated king, knight and bishop converge on the enemy king while guarding all possible escape squares. It's checkmate!

## CAPTURES

The complete rules of capturing (or "taking") are as follows:

1. You may capture any enemy piece (except the king) on any square to which one of your pieces can move, unless doing so would put yourself (or leave yourself) in check. The knight shown in Diagram 1.16 cannot capture White's queen on f6, because moving the knight would put Black's own king in check (by White's bishop on h3).

2. Pieces capture in the same way they move, except pawns, as explained earlier.

3. A king may capture an undefended piece, but can't be captured.

4. A capture is not compulsory, unless it's the only way out of check.

24

5. To make a capture, move your piece to a square occupied by one of your opponent's pieces, and remove the opponent's piece from the board. Only one piece can occupy a square at any given time.

6. You cannot capture your own men under any circumstances.

7. Only one capture can be made per move. The capturing piece must stop at the square on which the capture took place.

8. Captured men never return to the game, except when a pawn promotes.

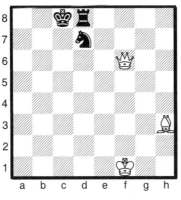

**Diagram 1.16**

The knight on d7 can't move, since doing so would expose his own king to check. This knight is **pinned**.

Take a look at Diagram 1.17, and ponder the following questions: Which pieces could capture which other pieces if it's White's turn to move? How about if it's Black to move? Once you identify a capture, try imagining what would happen next. Hint: Pieces not only attack enemy pieces, but also defend their own. Try to judge whether or not each capture is a good move. This exercise will help you begin to imagine future positions.

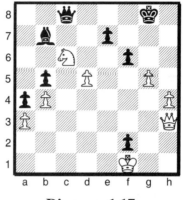

**Diagram 1.17**

**Q:** An unprotected piece that is attacked is said to be "hanging." Which pieces are hanging?
**A:** White's queen on h3; Black's pawns on e7 and f2.

## THE SET-UP

To start a game, the pieces must be set as shown in Diagram 1.18.

**1.** Pieces are placed along the edge of the board with letters on it. If your chessboard isn't labeled, just remember the term **light on right**. There must always be a light square on each player's nearest right hand corner.

**2.** White pieces are always set up along the 1st and 2nd ranks, and black pieces along the 7th and 8th ranks. The reason for this will become clear in Chapter 4.

**3.** The queen begins on a square of her own color. At the start of a game, the white queen stands on a light square, and the black queen stands on a dark square.

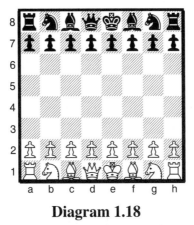

**Diagram 1.18**
Let the battle begin! But wait...

Three Things You Still Need to Know:

**1.** White always makes the first move.

**2.** Players take turns, moving one piece on each turn, except when castling (see Chapter 2).

**3.** You may not skip a turn. You must make a move when it's your turn if any legal move can be made.

# CHAPTER 1: REVIEW QUESTIONS:

1. What is a rank?
2. What is a file?
3. Which is the strongest chess piece and why?
4. Which is the most important chess piece and why?
5. What happens to a pawn when it reaches the far end of the board?
6. When can a king be captured?
7. What's it called when a king is threatened with immediate capture?
8. How do you win a chess game?
9. What does "light on right" mean?
10. What are the three ways to get out of check?

# 2. CASTLING, DRAWS, AND THE TOUCH-MOVE RULE

## CASTLING

Castling is a special move involving both king and rook. It's the only time a player moves two pieces in a single turn, and the only time a king moves two spaces at once.

When the pieces between the king and *one* rook have moved out of the way, as they have for White in Diagram 2.1, the player may castle by moving the king two squares toward the rook, then bringing the rook around, and next to, the king (Diagram 2.2).

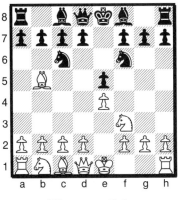

**Diagram 2.1**
White's position before castling

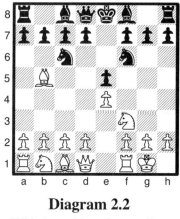

**Diagram 2.2**
White's position after castling

A player may castle on either side of the board. The previous two diagrams illustrate castling **kingside** (the side of the board on which the king starts the game). Diagrams 2.3 and 2.4 show a position before and after White castles **queenside**.

The technique remains the same: The king still moves two squares (toward the other rook) when castling queenside, but the rook takes a slightly longer walk to reach the other side of its king. This is why castling queenside is also known as **castling long**, and kingside castling is sometimes called **castling short**.

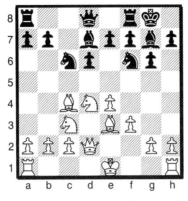

**Diagram 2.3**

White may castle to either side from this position

**Diagram 2.4**

White decides to castle queenside. Black had already castled kingside.

Why castle? I thought you'd never ask. Early in the game, your king is usually safer—harder to checkmate—when nearer the corner, since the battle is fought mainly toward the center. Castling also **develops** one of your rooks by bringing it nearer to the center. In roughly nine out of ten master-level games, both players castle, usually within the first ten moves. Castling represents the king's special ability to flee to temporary safety, symbolic of stepping inside his castle. It's often best not to advance the pawns in front of your castled king, unless there's some specific reason why you should. These pawns form a wall in front of your king, offering extra protection from enemy pieces. This wall of pawns is known as a **pawn shield**.

Castling is subject to a number of restrictions. The following is a list of situations in which a player is forbidden to castle:

**1.** A player may not castle unless all the squares between the rook and king are empty. A capture cannot be made while castling.

**2.** Castling can only be played from the original starting position of both rook and king.

**3.** If either your rook or king has moved at all, you may not castle for the rest of that game, even if those pieces return to their original squares. But if only one rook has moved, and not the king, you can still castle using the other rook.

**4.** You may not castle when your king is in check. In Diagram 2.5, the black king is in check, and may not castle to get out of check.

**5.** A player may not castle into check. As discussed earlier, you may not place your own king in jeopardy.

**6.** A castling king may not even pass through an attacked square. In Diagram 2.5, White cannot castle, because the enemy bishop attacks the f1 square. A king may not castle "through check."

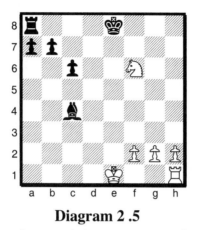

**Diagram 2 .5**

By the way, any attack on a rook does not prevent a player from castling.

**7.** When castling, you must first move the king two squares, then the rook. If you move the rook first, you are making a legal rook move (see the **touch-move rule** later this chapter). You may not move both pieces simultaneously.

## TYPES OF DRAWS

A tied game in chess is called a **draw**. There are seven ways in which a chess game can end in a draw. These are important to know, and will come in especially handy when you're losing.

**1. Agreement.** A player may offer a draw at any time during the game. If the opponent accepts the offer, the game ends in a tie. If you wish to offer a draw, you should do so right after you make a move. The offer stays in effect until your opponent accepts it, declines it, or makes his or her move (equal to declining). It's considered bad sportsmanship to offer a draw when you're obviously losing, or to make excessive draw offers.

**2. Stalemate.** This is a situation where the game is tied because the player whose move it is has no legal moves, but his king is not in check (Diagram 2. 6). If you find yourself behind by a queen or more, pray for stalemate. But if you're the other player, be careful. A tie game can be very disappointing for the player who had an easy win.

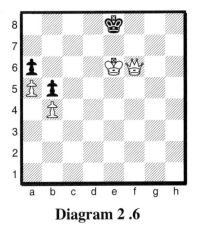

**Diagram 2 .6**
It's Black to move, unfortunately for White.

**3. Insufficient Mating Material.** This means neither player has enough forces to checkmate the opponent. If both players have only a king, for instance, checkmate can never be accomplished, so the game is drawn. Other examples of insufficient mating material are king and knight vs. king, and king and bishop vs. king. King and one pawn vs. king may be sufficient, because a pawn can promote. King and two knights vs. king are also sufficient, though the mate can never be forced. King, knight and bishop vs. king can force checkmate, but it's really, really hard to do!

**4. Three-Time Repetition.** If the same position is repeated three times (they need not be consecutive), with the same player to move each time, either player may claim the draw. This usually requires that the game be recorded (chapter 4). Otherwise, the claim is difficult to prove.

**5. The 50-Move Rule.** If each player has made fifty moves with NO pawn moves and NO captures, either player may claim the draw. For example, let's say you're playing with a king, one knight, and one bishop against a lone king. You have fifty moves (from the last capture or pawn move) to force checkmate, or the game will end in a draw. This claim also requires that the game be recorded.

**6. Perpetual Check.** This is a particular case of either the fifty-move rule, or three-time repetition. Simply keep checking the enemy king until either rule applies, whichever comes first. Diagram 2.7 shows an example in which White, about to get checkmated, finds a draw by perpetual check: the white queen can check the black king forever by moving to h6 and back to g6 indefinitely. Black's only legal reply would be to move the king back and forth between g8 and f8. Very soon the position will repeat itself three times, and the game will be drawn.

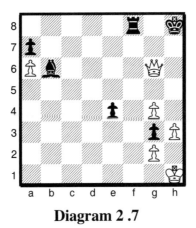

**Diagram 2 .7**

If White is foolish enough to stop giving check,
Black can move the rook to f1, checkmate!

7. **Adjudication.** When a game must be stopped before it's over, an appointed referee may examine the position and question the players to determine the most probable outcome, which could be a win for either side or a draw.

## THE TOUCH-MOVE RULE

1. If it's your move and you touch any of your pieces, you must move the first piece that you touched, if it has any legal move.

2. If it's your move and you touch one of your opponent's pieces, you must capture that piece if possible.

3. If you make a legal move and take your hand off the piece, it stays there, and counts as your move. Remember this when castling.

4. There is no penalty for touching a piece that has no legal moves, or for touching an opponent's piece that cannot be captured.

5. If an illegal move is made, it must be taken back, and another move made, with the same piece if possible.

6. If you touch a piece by accident, knocking it over or brushing against it, for instance, no penalty will ensue.

7. If a piece is off center and you want to adjust it, you must say "I adjust" before you touch the piece, in order to avoid having to move the piece. Adjustments can only be made by the player whose turn it is to move. Traditionally, chess players say, *"J'adoube,"* (French for "I adjust.")

Basically, a piece should not be touched by anyone when a game is in progress, other than the player whose turn it is to move, and even then, only when making a move or adjusting a piece. Touch-move is a rule, not an option.

Repeated, unnecessary touching of the pieces is considered bad sportsmanship. Other examples of bad sportsmanship include distracting your opponent, gloating, and refusing to shake your opponent's hand when the game is over. Chess players always shake hands at the end of a game.

# CHAPTER 2: REVIEW QUESTIONS

**1.** Which piece moves first when castling?

**2.** How does castling help your king?

**3.** How does castling help your rook?

**4.** What is stalemate?

**5.** What is perpetual check?

**6.** What happens if it's your move and you touch your opponent's knight?

**7.** What happens if a player makes an illegal move?

**8.** When may you touch a piece without having to move it?

**9.** When may a player touch a piece?

**10.** What do you do when a game ends?

# 3. PIECE VALUES AND THE EN PASSANT CAPTURE

## RELATIVE VALUES OF THE PIECES

Each piece has been assigned a standard numerical value to signify its power. These values are only guidelines, but are essentially reliable when sizing up your forces, or deciding whether or not to make a trade. The king has infinite value and never leaves the board, so it isn't counted when evaluating forces. The approximate values of the rest of the pieces are as follows:

**Queen** = 9
**Rook** = 5
**Bishop** = 3
**Knight** = 3
**Pawn** = 1

## COUNTING BY VALUE

New players often size up their positions by counting the number of pieces on each side, as if all pieces carry equal weight. Some of today's greatest players used to think that if you give up your queen and get a pawn for it, you've made an even trade, since each player gets one piece. But they soon learned that some pieces are more valuable than others.

To see who is ahead in **material**, just add up the total value of each of your pieces, and compare that number with the total value of your opponent's pieces. Counting is easiest when you start with the strongest piece(s) and work your way down. In Diagram 3.1, White has a rook (worth 5), a knight (3), and three pawns (1 each). 5 + 3 + 1+1+1 = 11. So White has a **piece count** of eleven. Black has a bishop (3), a knight (also 3), and four pawns (each worth 1). Black's piece count is ten (3+3+1+1+1+1). White is slightly ahead in material.

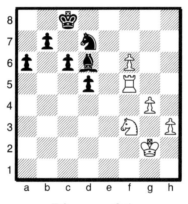

**Diagram 3.1**

White has an extra rook (5), which is slightly more than
Black's extra bishop and pawn (4).

## COUNTING BY COMPARISON

A more sophisticated approach to sizing up the strength of your army against that of your opponent's is comparing forces. Again, it's best to start with the strongest pieces and work your way down. Let's compare the armies of Diagram 3.2. Remember, kings don't count. Each player has a queen and one rook. What about bishops? Black has one bishop and White has no bishops. At this point in our comparison, Black leads by a bishop. This is more specific than saying, "Black is ahead by three," which could mean an extra bishop, or an extra knight, or three extra pawns, or even and extra rook that cost two pawns to get. Instead, we know that Black has a bishop and White doesn't. How about knights? Black has one, but White has two. So White has an extra knight (3) to compensate for Black's extra bishop (3). As for pawns, each player has five. Material is even.

Comparing forces is tricky at first, but well worth the trouble, since it provides more detailed information about the imbalances in your position. In Diagram 3.2, White has an extra knight where Black has an extra bishop. Each is worth 3, but White's knight can jump over pieces, while Black's bishop can fly across the board in a single leap, attacking squares from far away.

## TRADING

An exchange of knights, for instance, is an even trade of material, but which side will benefit more from this trade depends on the position. An "even" trade is almost never equally good for both sides. In Diagram 3.2, it's White's move. If White's knight on e4 captures Black's knight on f6, with check, Black can recapture with the pawn on g7 or the bishop. This may look like an even trade at first glance, but once Black's knight has been removed from f6, White can use the queen to take the pawn on h7, checkmate!

**Diagram 3.2**

Black's knight is busy guarding h7.
White trades knights to remove the defender.

Also remember, when considering a trade, that the value of a piece depends on its positioning in relation to other pieces. In Diagram 3.3 material is even, but Black can't stop White's pawn on f7 from queening.

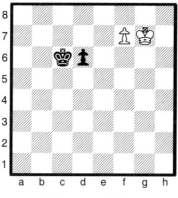

**Diagram 3.3**

In this position, the black pawn is worth a pawn.
The white pawn is worth a queen! Black would LOVE
to trade a pawn for a pawn here, but can't.

Take a look at Diagram 3.4, and consider which is stronger: White's rook or Black's rook? White's bishop or Black's bishop? White's knight or Black's knight? Hint: To find out which of each pair has more scope, count all the squares to which each piece could move at this time, regardless of whether or not the move is a good one.

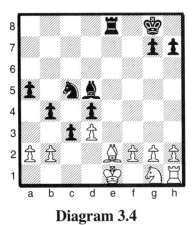

**Diagram 3.4**

White's rook has no moves (it's entombed), nor does White's bishop (it's pinned). Even White's knight has very limited scope. What's more, Black's pawns, which defend each other, are dangerously close to queening. Material is even, but not for long. Black has the much better game here, and should soon win.

## THE RELATIVE VALUE OF KNIGHTS AND BISHOPS

A knight and a bishop are each worth three, so which is stronger? Again, the value of a piece depends on its position and its scope. Positional judgment takes practice, but let's begin by comparing knights and bishops. Bishops have long-range capabilities, while knights make short, clumsy moves. On the other hand, a bishop may visit only half the squares on a chessboard (one color only), where a knight can attack any square. Also, bishops can be blocked by other pieces, while knights can jump right over them. So which is stronger, a knight or a bishop? The answer is, "It depends," and is often a question of personal taste and playing style. Which do you like better?

## THE EN PASSANT CAPTURE

**En Passant** (pronounced ON-pass-ONt) is a French term meaning "in passing." The en passant capture is a special pawn capture that only occurs under certain conditions. It is not mandatory, and it is not necessarily a good move. It is simply an available option that could come in handy.

Suppose a pawn is standing on its own 5th rank—that is, five ranks from the edge of the board behind the pawn—as in Diagram 3.5.

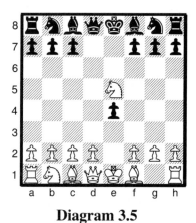

**Diagram 3.5**

A black pawn has found its way to e4 (its own 5th rank).

Then, suppose the enemy pawn on either adjacent file moves two squares forward, so that it stands right next to the above-mentioned pawn, as if trying to avoid being captured by it. For instance, the white pawn in Diagram 3.6 has just moved from d2 to d4.

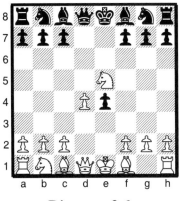

**Diagram 3.6**

White's d-pawn escapes being captured by Black's e-pawn... or does it?

When this happens, the pawn that stands on its own 5th rank may capture the pawn that has just moved two squares, by passing it. In other words, a pawn that has just moved two squares can be captured by another pawn as if it had only moved one square (Diagram 3.7).

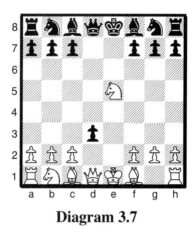

**Diagram 3.7**

The black e4 pawn has captured the white d4 pawn en passant.
Black removed the white pawn from d4,
but the capturing pawn landed on d3.

All of the following rules apply to the en passant capture:

1. When a pawn moves two squares (and immediately next to an enemy pawn) the en passant capture can only be played on that very move, or not at all. The same pawn cannot be captured en passant on any later move.

2. The pawn being captured en passant has to have just made its first move (two squares forward).

3. The en passant capture can be played to either side. Back in Diagram 3.5, if White had played a pawn to f4 instead of d4, the black e5 pawn could still have captured en passant, landing on f3.

4. Only pawns may capture, or be captured, en passant.

## CHAPTER 3: REVIEW QUESTIONS

**1.** Which is generally stronger—a queen or two rooks?

**2.** What makes a chess piece strong (or weak)?

**3.** Normally, would you trade your rook for a bishop?

**4.** How is a knight superior to a bishop?

**5.** How is a bishop superior to a knight?

**6.** What pieces are involved in the en passant capture?

**7.** When can a pawn be captured en passant?

**8.** Can the white d-pawn capture the black h-pawn en passant?

**9.** White has a queen, two knights, and six pawns. Black has two rooks, two bishops, and three pawns. Who is ahead in material, and by how much?

**10.** Can a pawn make an en passant capture and promote on the same move?

# 4. THE LANGUAGE OF CHESS

In order to learn, teach, or even talk about chess, we need to communicate positions and move sequences. In chapter 1, we discussed algebraic notation. Naming squares in this way is a shortcut that allows you to say, for instance, "e7" instead of "seven squares up from the lower left hand corner, then five squares over to the right." See how much time that saves?

**THE PIECES**

For recording a whole move, a further shorthand device is needed. In written (English) chess notation, each piece is represented by a capital letter, except the pawn, which is not mentioned in algebraic notation. The pieces are represented by the following capital letters:

**King** = K
**Queen** = Q
**Rook** = R
**Bishop** = B
**Knight** = N (because "**K**" is for king)

In Diagram 4.1, White's e-pawn, the one on the e-file, in front of the king, advanced two squares on its first move. Conventionally, we call this move **e4**, and not *Pe4* (though there is no harm in writing *Pe4*, since its meaning is perfectly clear). Black's first move was **e6** (not *Pe6*). Then White played **d4,** and Black played **d5**. Then the white bishop moved to the d3 square. To describe this move, you could say "bishop d3," or write **Bd3**. In other words, just name the piece (unless it's a pawn) and its destination square.

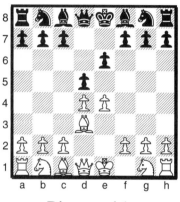

**Diagram 4.1**

1) e4; e6 2) d4; d5 3) Bd3 ... It's Black to move.
This opening is called the French Defense.

Always use lowercase letters when naming squares, and capital letters to signify pieces.

## CAPTURES

A capture is represented by a small letter x. Let's say your king captures (takes) a knight on the a4 square. The move can be stated as 'king takes a4." The same move written down would look like this: **Kxa4**. Notice that the piece being captured is not mentioned in algebraic notation, only the square on which the capture takes place. That's why the move is written as **Kxa4**, and not KxN, as in "king takes knight."

A pawn capture is written in pretty much the same way as any other capture, except that a pawn is identified by the letter of the file on which it stands. In Diagram 4.2, let's say the pawn on b6 takes the knight on c7. The written move would look like this: **bxc7** (The pawn on the b-file takes the piece on c7). The en passant capture is written in a similar way: In Diagrams 3.6 and 3.7 from the previous chapter, Black's pawn on e4 captured White's pawn on d4, en passant, thereby landing on d3. The same rules of notation apply here: Name the file of the pawn making the capture, and the square that it lands on. So the capture would be written like this: **exd3**. In other words, **e** (the e-pawn) **x** (takes) **d3** (in this case, the pawn that went to d4, en passant).

## Pawn Promotion

As we learned in chapter 1, a pawn always promotes to another piece once it reaches its farthest rank. For example, if a white pawn on d7 captures something on e8, making a queen, you would write it down this way: **dxe8=Q**.

## Castling

The written symbol for castling kingside (short) is **0-0**. Queenside (long) castling is written **0-0-0**.

## Check

A move that puts a king in check is usually followed by a plus sign (+), but some players like to use a checkmark. Either way is equally acceptable. Suppose your rook takes a piece on c7, and checks the enemy king from there. You could write it this way: **Rxc7+** (rook takes c7, check).

## Checkmate

The simplest way to write checkmate is to use a double plus sign (++). If your queen took something on h7, checkmating the enemy king, the last move on your score sheet might look like this: **Qxh7++** (queen takes h7, mate!).

## MORE SPECIFIC NOTATION

Look again at Diagram 4.2. Notice that White can take Black's bishop on e4 with either the knight on c3 or the knight on g5. In this case, writing Nxe4 is not clear enough, since it does not tell us which knight captures the piece on e4. Here, you would have to further identify the knight by naming its present file. In other words, you'd write **Ncxe4** (the knight on the c-file takes the piece on e4), or, if capturing with the other knight, then **Ngxe4** (the knight on the g-file takes the piece on e4).

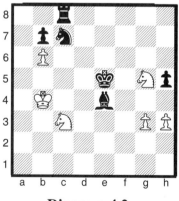

**Diagram 4.2**

White, to move, might try Ncxe4, or Ngxe4, or even bxc7.

Diagram 4.3 shows another example of more specific chess notation, this time involving two rooks. Notice that Black's pawn on c4 can be captured by either of White's rooks—the one on c6 or the one on c2. Both rooks stand on the c-file, but you can specify one of them by naming its present rank. Capturing the c4 pawn here would be written as **R6xc4** (the rook on the 6th rank takes on c4), or **R2xc4** (the rook on the 2nd rank takes on c4).

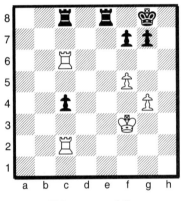

**Diagram 4.3**

White can capture Black's c-pawn with either rook, and then material will be even.

Systems for recording moves were developed for many practical reasons:

**1.** You can analyze your game after it's over (looking at your games, especially losses, is the best way to improve your skills).

**2.** When you win brilliantly, you can show the game to everyone.

**3.** You can track your improvement as a player over time.

**4.** You can enjoy the games of other players.

**5.** You can save a game you didn't have time to finish. It can be resumed any time.

**6.** Your game score can be used to reset the position if the pieces get messed up somehow, by playing it out from the beginning.

**7.** Your game score enables you to claim certain types of draws (see Chapter 2).

**8.** In official, rated tournaments, a score sheet is used in conjunction with a clock to ensure that each player makes the required number of moves within the allotted time. A player who oversteps the time limit without making enough moves forfeits the game. The opponent can use his/her score sheet as proof to claim the win.

On the next page is a partial illustration of a score sheet for recording a chess game. Each player must record the moves of both players. Names go at the top of the page, next to whichever color each player is using. White's moves go on the left, followed by Black's moves on the right. If you play out the moves from this game score, you will arrive at the position shown in Diagram 4.4.

**WHITE: Joe Smith**
**BLACK: Amy Chan**

|   | White | Black |
|---|-------|-------|
| 1 | e4    | e5    |
| 2 | Nf3   | Nc6   |
| 3 | Bb5   | a6    |
| 4 | Ba4   | Nf6   |
| 5 | O-O   | Be7   |
| 6 | Re1   | b5    |
| 7 | Bb3   | O-O   |

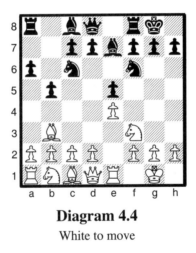

**Diagram 4.4**
White to move

When writing your moves, you can adjourn the game and resume it later simply by playing over the game from the beginning, using your score sheet. But even if your game isn't being recorded, you can still write down the current position. To do this, you need only write the color and location of each type of piece, and whose move it is. Writing "P" for pawn is fine when recording an adjourned position. Diagram

4.5 shows an adjourned position, which the players wrote down like this:

**White (to move):** K/e4 N/f4 P/b4, c5, c6
**Black:** K/e7 B/f7 P/a6, c7

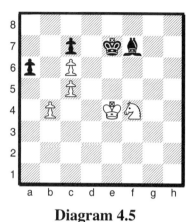

**Diagram 4.5**
A game was adjourned—and resumed—at this point,
because the position was recorded.

If a game is written properly, you should be able to re-enact it later. Going over your own games, especially your losses, is a very useful way to improve at chess.

Here's an example of the famous four-move checkmate called the **scholar's mate**, written in algebraic chess notation. Diagram 4.6 shows the final position.

|   | White | Black |
|---|-------|-------|
| 1 | e4    | e5    |
| 2 | Bc4   | Bc5   |
| 3 | Qh5   | Nf6   |
| 4 | Qxf7++ |      |

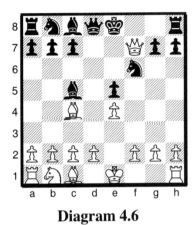

**Diagram 4.6**

White's queen and bishop cooperate to converge on f7. Black was developing pieces, but forgot to watch out for threats!

## CHAPTER 4: REVIEW QUESTIONS

1. What is the symbol that represents a knight in algebraic notation?

2. What type of letter refers to a file?

3. How would you write this move in algebraic notation: The knight on g4 captures a pawn on h6?

4. What would you write if a pawn on b3 took the queen on c4?

5. What does this move mean: **f8=N**?

6. Let's say you castle long, and your rook lands on a square where it attacks the enemy king. How do you write this move?

7. What are three good reasons for recording a game?

8. What does **gxh7++** mean?

9. Which of White's pieces are able to move after **1) e4**?

10. If a white rook goes to c1, attacking the queen on c7, how would you write this move?

# 5. THE CLOCK

You can't play chess competitively without knowing how to use a chess clock. Chess clocks are almost always used in tournaments, to give each player a certain length of time in which to make a certain number of moves. This is known as **time control**. Otherwise, a game could take forever.

An old style chess clock is a rectangular clock with two faces. On top of the clock are two buttons, one above each face. When one button is pressed, the clock on that side stops, and the other side runs. After each move, a player presses the button on his or her side. This way, your clock is only running when it's your turn to move—though it's a very smart idea to think on your opponent's time, too. The clock is stopped completely by pressing both buttons half way down.

The faces are identical, and look like ordinary clock faces, with one crucial exception. There's a small red flag hanging down from just to the left of each twelve. As the minute hand nears the hour mark, the flag begins to lift. When the minute hand hits twelve, it passes the flag, so the flag falls back down again.

Modern chess clocks are digital and follow the same principle as old style analog clocks, only digital clocks are programmed instead of wound, and they show liquid crystal displays (LCDs) rather than mechanical faces. Also, no flag is needed to capture the millisecond your time runs out. A digital clock will simply read zero (00:00).

Some time controls require each player to make a set number of moves within a set number of minutes. Others give each player a certain length of time for the entire game.

In a 30/90 (thirty-ninety) time control, for instance, each player has 90 minutes in which to make 30 moves. If you happen to make 30 moves in less than ninety minutes, you don't lose any of your time remaining. It simply carries over to the next time control. In 30/90 games, the clocks are usually set at 4:30, and you have to have made 30 moves by the time your flag falls when the clock says 6:00. The flag will also fall at 5:00, but you can ignore this in a 30/90 time control.

A moves/minutes time control is often followed by a **sudden death** time control. For example, in a 30/90 time control, once you've used your first 90 minutes and made at least 30 moves, you might have a set length of time, like 30 or 60 minutes to play the whole rest of the game, no matter how many more moves it takes.

A time control of "game sixty" (G/60) means each player has one hour to play the entire game from start to finish.

Similarly, G/30 means each player has 30 minutes to play the entire game.

In a G/5 time control, known as **blitz**, or **speed chess**, each player has five minutes to play the entire game. Yes, you read it right.

Here are some rules pertaining to chess clocks.

**1.** If you run out of time before meeting the move requirement, you forfeit the game, regardless of the position, unless your last move was checkmate.

**2.** You must notice and declare your opponent's time forfeit in order to claim the win. You do this simply by saying "Your flag's down," or something to that effect, and stopping the clock. If your opponent disagrees, call the tournament director. Score sheets are used as proof of how many moves have been played.

**3.** If you continue playing without noticing your opponent has run out of time, you may not be able to claim the win later. For instance, if you get checkmated, and *then* notice your opponent's flag was down, too bad.

**4.** Recording your moves is required in tournament competition, unless you have fewer than five minutes left on your clock.

**5.** If a player runs out of time, the opponent must already have an accurate score sheet. You may not claim a time-forfeit win by recording any more than three moves after the fact. Your score sheet must be playable and legible, with no more than three mistakes.

**6.** Some digital clocks have what's called a five-second time delay. This means that when you have less than two minutes on your clock, your clock will not start running until five seconds after your opponent has pressed it. This is to help prevent players from losing by time forfeit in clearly drawn or won positions. During your last two minutes, if you take less than five seconds to make each move, you will not lose any further time on your clock.

**7.** A corresponding rule applies to the analog clock: if you have less than two minutes left on your clock, you may be able to claim a **draw by no losing chances**. This means you stop the clocks, bring the tournament director to your game, and show the director how your game could not possibly be lost. For instance, if only kings remain, it's a draw by insufficient mating material. This rule is important, as you can imagine how annoying it would be if, say, only kings remained, and the player with more time could just march his king around and around until the player with less time forfeited.

**8.** If you forget to press your clock after you make your move, your opponent does not have to remind you, and nobody else is allowed to tell you. You can lose on time just waiting for your opponent to move. Check your time situation frequently to avoid this nightmare.

**9.** You have to press the clock with the same hand you used to make your move.

And finally, please note: chess clocks are expensive (at the time of this writing, costing anywhere from $50 to $250), and few people know how to fix them when they break. So be gentle with your clock. Don't slam it too hard when you play. Pack it carefully when you travel.

# 6. BASIC CHECKMATES

When you find yourself ahead by a rook or more, it's often best to trade off the remaining pieces until you end up with just your king and rook (or more) vs. your opponent's lone king. At this point, forcing checkmate is only a matter of technique. This chapter offers step-by-step instruction on delivering checkmate to a lone king, using various extra forces. Keep in mind the following principles:

**1.** No piece is able to force checkmate all by itself. At least one other piece is needed, either to defend the first piece or to guard or block the enemy king's escape squares.

**2.** Usually, a king must be driven to the edge, sometimes a corner, of the board in order to be checkmated.

**3.** If you have only your king left with no pawns on the board, head for the center. A king is much harder to checkmate in the center.

## KING AND TWO ROOKS VS. KING

Your rooks can work together to drive the enemy king to an edge. Each rook attacks an entire row of squares, forming a kind of "fence" in front of the king, which stops it from advancing. When the whole row in front of the opponent's king is guarded by one of your rooks, you can attack the next row with your other rook, forcing the king to retreat. For a complete demonstration of this technique, see Diagrams 6.1 thru 6.5.

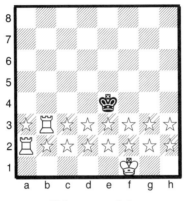

**Diagram 6.1**

Some of each rook's attack squares are marked with stars.
Black's king is fenced in.

Notice each rook's attack squares. Of course rooks also attack vertically, but the important guarded squares here are the ones fencing in the enemy king. White's first move here can cut off another row of squares, driving the Black king further back (Diagram 6.2).

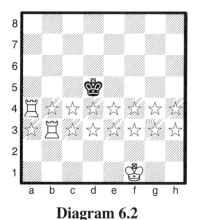

**Diagram 6.2**

Ra4+ forces the Black king back (to d5, perhaps).
White's rook on b3 stopped it from advancing.

What's White's best move now? If you said "**Rb5+**"
you've been paying attention! **Rb5+** cuts off another row of
squares from Black's king, driving it back again, perhaps to
c6 (see Diagram 6.3). But now White is faced with a problem. Black's king is threatening to capture White's undefended rook on b5!

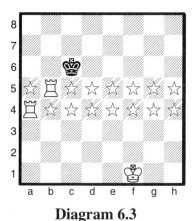

**Diagram 6.3**

A king, working alone, can still make threats.

When this happens, the threatened rook should move as far away from the enemy king as possible, while staying on the same rank. This way, the enemy king can still not advance. What should White play now (see caption of Diagram 6.4)?

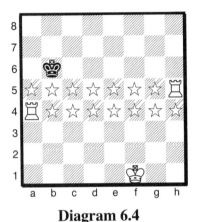

**Diagram 6.4**

Rh5 does the trick, escaping attack without allowing Black's king to advance. Black's best reply is ...Kb6.

White was threatening **Ra6+**, driving the black king back again. But the king, not one to give up so easily, played . . . **Kb6**, which stops **Ra6+** in its tracks, since Black's king could now capture the rook if it went to a6. So White plays **Rg4** (Diagram 6.5), once again avoiding attack without retreating.

Notice how the rooks occupy different files, so they don't prevent each other from advancing. Rh4 instead of Rg4 would have been a mistake.

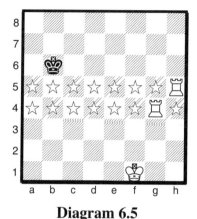

**Diagram 6.5**

No matter what Black does now, White will play Rg6,
then Rh7, then Rg8+ +.

## KING AND QUEEN VS. KING

You can force checkmate quickly if your king and queen cooperate. In Diagram 6.6, some of the queen's attack squares are marked with stars. Notice that these squares form a box around the Black king, restricting its movement. White's job is to 1) make this box increasingly smaller until the enemy king is forced to an edge, and 2) move the king forward to protect its queen. What's White's best move here?

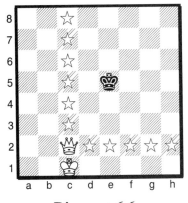

**Diagram 6.6**

This queen, with the help of her king, will drive the Black
king to an edge and checkmate it.

If you said **Qc4**, good work! The box becomes smaller,
and the queen is safe when placed a "knight's distance" away
from the enemy king. Then Black might play, say, **Kf5**, and
we arrive at the position shown in Diagram 6.7.

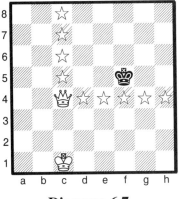

**Diagram 6.7**

Black is helpless. White has plenty of time to walk the king up to
where it supports the queen.

Starting from the position shown in Diagram 6.7, the game might continue like this:

| | White | Black |
|---|---|---|
| 1 | Kd2 | Ke5 |
| 2 | Ke3 | Kf5 |
| 3 | Qe4+ | |

The queen is defended by her king.

| | | |
|---|---|---|
| 3 | ... | Kg5 |
| 4 | Qf4+ | Kg6 |
| 5 | Ke4 | Kg7 |
| 6 | Qd6! | |

Controls the 6th rank, trapping the enemy king on the 7th & 8th ranks.

| | | |
|---|---|---|
| 6 | ... | Kf7 |
| 7 | Kf5 | Kg7 |
| 8 | Qf6+ | Kg8 |

...which brings us to the position shown in Diagram 6.8, with White to move.

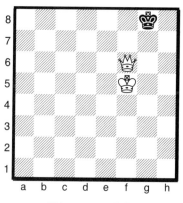

**Diagram 6.8**

Once the enemy king is forced to the back rank, trap him there once and for all.

68

White has to hold the black king to the edge of the board, always being careful not to cause a draw by stalemate. **Qe7** is best here, guarding the entire 7th rank (Kg6 would have been stalemate!). Now the Black king can do nothing to stop White from closing in. Black cannot even threaten White's queen (he'd be putting himself in check). After **Qe7**, White cannot be stopped from playing **Kg6** or **Kf6**, followed by **Qg7**, mate. If a queen is defended by its own king, it cannot be captured by the enemy king. Remember, when attacking a lone king, to watch out for stalemate! If you want to play a move that is not check, be sure your opponent will be able to move after you do.

## KING AND ROOK VS. KING

As usual, the lone king must be driven to an edge. White's rook and king work together to accomplish this. To see how it's done, set up the position shown in Diagram 6.9.

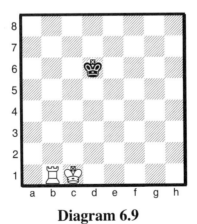

**Diagram 6.9**

White's king and rook will work as partners to
force mate on Black's king.

White should start by fencing in the Black king as much as possible with **Rb5**. Then Black, unwilling to retreat but unable to advance, might play **Kc6**, threatening White's rook (Diagram 6.10).

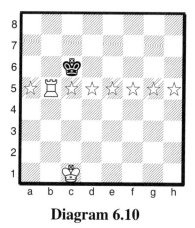

**Diagram 6.10**

Black's king is already restricted to three ranks, but White still has to be careful.

The enemy king must be stopped from advancing, and cannot be allowed to capture the rook. Play out the following moves (starting from Diagram 6.10), and read the **annotations**. When you are finished, you should have the position in Diagram 6.11.

| | White | Black |
|---|---|---|
| **1** | **Rh5** | |

Staying on the rank while avoiding capture.

| | White | Black |
|---|---|---|
| **1** | ... | **Kd6** |
| **2** | **Kd2** | |

The rook can't do it alone!

| | White | Black |
|---|---|---|
| **2** | ... | **Ke6** |

| 3 | Ke3 | Kf6 |
| 4 | Kf4 | Kg6 |
| 5 | Ra5 | |

See comment on move 1.

| 5 | ... | Kf6 |
| 6 | Ra6+ | ... |

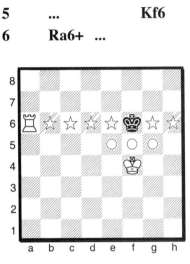

**Diagram 6.11**

When one king faces the other with one square between them,
neither king can advance.

Here, the important squares guarded by White's king are marked with circles, and some of the squares guarded by White's rook are marked with stars. Notice that, since the kings are directly facing each other, the white king stops the black king from advancing. What this means is that the white rook's services on the 5th rank are no longer needed, and it is free to take over the next rank. See how **Ra6+** drives the black king backward? If not for the white king, the black king would be able to advance, avoiding the fatal edge. Starting from Diagram 6.11 (it's Black's move), the game might continue like this:

| | White | Black |
|---|---|---|
| 6 | ... | Ke7 |
| 7 | Ke5 | Kf7 |

White is faced with a new problem here. Whenever his king gets *in front* of the black king, the black king just steps to one side. White wants his king to face the black king when it's White's turn to move. If White plays **Ra7+** now, Black could play **Kg6**, escaping toward the center. So White makes a **waiting move**: an insignificant move with no meaningful effect on the position, except to change whose move it is.

| 8 | Rb6 |
|---|---|

White keeps the rook on the 6th rank, still a comfortable distance away from Black's king, without giving up any space. Now Black must move somewhere. If he plays **Ke7**, facing White's king with White to move, White will play **Rb7+**, driving Black's king to the edge. So let's say Black tries **Kg7** instead. White will then follow Black's king to the side, where the lone king will then be forced to face the attacking king. The game might end this way:

| 8 | ... | Kg7 |
|---|---|---|
| 9 | Kf5 | Kh7 |
| 10 | Kg5 | Kg7 |
| 11 | Rb7+ | Kf8 |
| 12 | Kg6 | Ke8 |
| 13 | Kf6 | Kd8 |
| 14 | Ke6 | Kc8 |
| 15 | Rh7 | |

Pausing to get out of the way!

| 15 | ... | Kb8 |
|----|-----|-----|
| 16 | Kd6 | Ka8 |
| 17 | Kc6 | Kb8 |
| 18 | Rg7 | |

A waiting move.

| 18 | ... | Ka8 |
|----|-----|-----|
| 19 | Kb6 | |

Forcing Black to face the music.

| 19 | ... | Kb8 |
|----|-----|-----|
| 20 | Rg8++ | |

To sum it all up, there are four parts to this technique:

**1.** Cutting off space with the rook.

**2.** Bringing the king forward to face the other king, in order to stop it from advancing.

**3.** Keeping the rook safe without retreating.

**4.** Making waiting moves so the rook can give check when the kings are facing each other.

All it takes is a little practice.

For more experienced players, it's considered bad sportsmanship not to resign the game when you are hopelessly lost. However, if you're a beginner, take heart! All is not hopelessly lost. It's possible that your opponent hasn't yet learned the proper technique to force checkmate on a lone king. If you play on, you can still hope for a draw by stalemate, insufficient mating material, three-time repetition, or, in some cases, the 50- move rule.

## CHAPTER 6: REVIEW QUESTIONS

1. What is the minimum number of pieces required to force checkmate?
2. On which part of the chessboard is it most difficult to force checkmate?
3. How does a lone king fight back against a king and rook?
4. When forcing mate with two rooks vs. king, why must the rooks be on different files?
5. How does a king help his queen to force checkmate?
6. When both kings face each other on the same file with one square between them, what do they prevent each other from doing?
7. If your lone king directly faces the other king as described in Question 6, but your opponent also has a rook, whose move do you want it to be?
8. What is a waiting move?
9. If you have a king and pawn vs. your opponent's lone king, is it possible to force checkmate?
10. What are two ways in which a lone king can draw against a king and queen?

# 7. OPENING STRATEGY

The **opening** is the first part of a chess game. **Strategy**, a word of military origin, refers to the plans you make to get an advantage over your adversary. Chess strategies are not individual moves, but overall goals for your position that may take a number of moves to achieve. In this chapter we learn about four main opening strategies, and every opening move you make should meet, or prepare to meet, at least one of these goals:

1. Develop your pieces,
2. Attack center squares,
3. Castle (or not, but get your king safe!), and
4. Look for threats.

## DEVELOPMENT

To have the best chance of winning, you must get your stronger pieces out as early as possible. These are the forces you fight with, as similar forces are fighting against you. If a boxer tried to save one of his fists for a later round, there wouldn't be a later round. It's usually advisable to bring out your knights and bishops first, followed by your rooks and queen. Get them all developed. Notice that in order to move either of your bishops, you must first move a pawn out of its way. Diagram 7.1 shows an opening position where both players have developed their knights and bishops. Each player has taken only seven moves to do this.

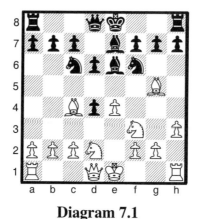

**Diagram 7.1**

Both players still need to castle, and to bring out
their rooks and queens.

Beginners are often advised not to bring the queen out early. The reason for this principle is that, sometimes, your opponent can develop pieces and attack your queen at the same time. You might find yourself so busy whisking her off to safety that you don't get a chance to bring out the rest of your pieces. Don't be afraid of developing your queen early, but think carefully about where it should go. In Diagram 7.2, both players have developed their queens to safe squares, where they will likely become useful.

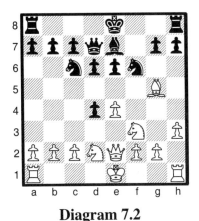

**Diagram 7.2**
Actually, this is a continuation of the game shown in Diagram 7.1.

Development is important because there is strength in numbers. Your whole army working together is stronger than the sum of its parts. If an army of soldiers attacked you, what chance would you have of defeating them all by yourself, or by sending in one soldier at a time? Once your pieces are developed, they can cooperate with each other to attack enemy pieces and defend their own. Developed pieces have more moves, and are therefore stronger than those that are undeveloped. The more mobility a piece has, the stronger that piece is. But from the starting point of a chess game, only knights and pawns have any moves at all. Part of your job in the opening is to free your pieces so they can zoom around the board.

---

**Helpful Hint:**
You may remember learning that pieces tend to have more scope when placed toward the center, than when placed on a corner or an edge. In fact, most of the fighting takes place near the center of the board. For this reason, it's suggested that you develop your pieces so they aim toward center squares. For instance, if you want to bring out your knight on the first move, **1) Nf3**, attacking d4 and e5, is a much better move than **1) Nh3**. Similarly, **1) Nc3**, aiming at d5 and e4, is superior to **1) Na3**.

---

## FIGHTING FOR THE CENTER

The **center** refers to the four squares right smack in the middle of the board—d4, d5, e4, and e5. These are marked with stars in Diagram 7.3. The squares surrounding the center (marked here with circles) are known as the **expanded center**.

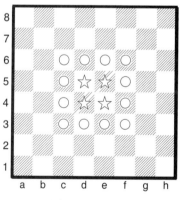

**Diagram 7.3**
You'd like to put your pieces on center squares,
but so would your opponent.

A piece that attacks a square is often said to be fighting for control of that square. To control a square means to guard it well enough so an enemy piece that goes there will be lost. The more squares you control, the stronger your pieces become. Center squares are the most valuable squares to control in opening and middle game play, though squares of the expanded center are also useful. Diagram 7.4 shows a position where both players have developed pieces and pawns while fighting for control of center squares.

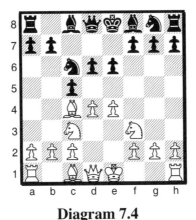

**Diagram 7.4**

In this position, every move made so far attacks
at least one center square.

In opening and middle game play, it's especially important to control as many squares as possible on your opponent's half of the board, also known as your opponent's **territory**. In Diagram 7.4, White's pieces attack eight squares in Black's territory—a6, b5, c5, d5, e5, f5, g5, and h6. Black's pieces attack only three squares in White's territory—b4, d4, and h4. Therefore, White has what's known as a **spatial advantage**. The more squares you attack in your opponent's territory, the more pressure your opponent's army has to endure, and the more mobility for your own pieces.

## CASTLING

By now you've learned that castling makes your king safer by moving it further away from the fighting that goes on in the center. Also, that castling brings one of your rooks toward the center, where it is better able to join the fight. So castling is a multi-purpose move, aiding in the development of a strong piece and protecting the king. No one has to castle, but it is considered an excellent opening strategy, and often a necessary part of opening development.

## THREATS

Looking for threats is a good strategy at any stage of the game. If several moves look equally good to you, play the move that makes the biggest threat, provided you are not being seriously threatened yourself. For a simple example of this concept, see Diagram 7.5.

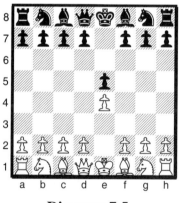

**Diagram 7.5**
White has many moves to choose from here.

It's White's turn to move. He might try **2) Nc3, 2) Bc4**, or **2) Nf3**. Each of these moves develops a piece, attacks one or more center squares, and (maybe) prepares to castle. But **2) Nf3** is considered a sharper move than the other two, because it also threatens to take the e5 pawn. Though the pawn is easily defended, the more threats you make, the more likely your opponent will blunder. Always look for threats! And remember, both players make threats. Whoever is making the threats at any given time is said to have the **initiative**. Wasting time on useless moves will give your opponent the initiative, so make every move count!

These four main opening strategies can be seen as a checklist. For every opening move, you should be able to answer "yes" to at least one, and preferably more than one, question on the list. Set up the starting position (Diagram 7.6), and let's look at some first moves for White:

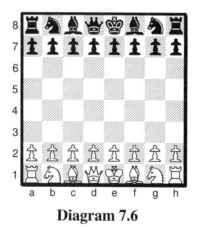

**Diagram 7.6**

White starts the game slightly ahead in time, since White moves first. This is why most players prefer White. But don't let it psych you out! Black wins about half of all decisive (not drawn) games.

Suppose White plays **1) e4**.

**Q:** Does the move help to develop any pieces?

**A:** Yes. **1) e4** allows the bishop on f1 and the queen on d1 to move.

**Q:** Does the move attack any center squares?

**A:** Yes. The pawn on e4 attacks d5 (not to mention f5).

**Q:** Does the move help prepare to castle?

**A:** Yes, if White wants to castle kingside, since the f1 bishop can now move.

**Q:** Does the move make a threat?

**A:** No, but neither does any other first move for White.

Based on these results, **1) e4** looks like an excellent first move for White, since it answers yes to three out of four questions on the openings checklist.

But what if White plays a move like **1) a3**?

**Q:** Does it develop any pieces?

**A:** No. Where would the rook go from a2?

**Q:** Does it attack any center squares?

**A:** No. It has no effect on the center.

**Q:** Does it help prepare to castle?

**A:** No. White could castle just as easily without playing it.

**Q:** Does it make a threat?

**A:** No.

According to our checklist, **1) a3** is an inferior first move for White. It wastes precious time and there are so many more useful moves to play! A unit of time in chess, an extra move, is called a **tempo**. If you develop and make threats at the same time, your opponent may be too busy defending those threats to develop his own army. Games have been won by a single tempo! White starts one tempo ahead by having the first move. A useless move like **1) a3** throws away that extra tempo. It's a bit like letting Black go first.

How about **1) Nh3**?

**Q:** Does it develop any pieces?

**A:** Yes. It develops a knight.

**Q:** Does it attack any center squares?

**A:** No. This knight would have been better placed on f3.

**Q:** Does it help prepare to castle?

**A:** Yes, if White should castle kingside.

**Q:** Does it make a threat?

**A:** No.

It seems that **1) Nh3** satisfies only two out of four checklist requirements, so it may not be the best first move for White. If you think about this checklist on every move throughout the opening (including your opponent's moves ), your army will be much better prepared for the middle game fight, and you'll be more likely to notice your opponent's mistakes.

## CHAPTER 7: REVIEW QUESTIONS

**1.** What is the opening?

**2.** What is development?

**3.** What is the center?

**4.** Why is it usually preferable to develop pieces toward the center?

**5.** What is the expanded center?

**6.** What does it mean to attack a square (or a piece)?

**7.** What does it mean to control a square?

**8.** What is a spatial advantage?

**9.** What is the initiative?

**10.** What is a tempo?

# 8. MIDDLE GAME STRATEGY

Around the time both players have developed their **minor pieces**, knights and bishops, and castled, the position reaches a point called the **middle game**. In the opening, you stationed your men on squares where they would be best able to attack, and brought your king to safety. The middle game is usually when the real fighting begins. Pieces are traded, rooks and queens become more active, and the opposing forces attack and capture each other in trying to reach the enemy king.

The middle game is the most confusing part of a chess game, and the possibilities are endless, so there's no point in trying to figure them all out. Rather, there are certain basic strategies you can use to guide you through any position. This chapter covers five important middle game strategies:

**1.** Rook development
**2.** Coordination
**3.** Exploiting weaknesses
**4.** Attacking the king
**5.** Defense

## ROOK DEVELOPMENT

Rooks are best placed on open files. An **open file** is a file with no pawns on it. Rooks are often blocked by their own pawns. One good way to help develop a rook is to castle, bringing it toward the center. Another is to capture something with a pawn, creating an open file, and then placing a rook on that file. You see, when a pawn makes a capture, it moves to another file, opening a line of squares for a rook to move around on. If you can't get an open file, another good place for your rook might be a **half-open file**—a file with just your opponent's pawn(s) on it. A file with both players' pawns on it is called a **closed file**, and is not usually considered the best place for your rooks. To show how rooks become active, see Diagram 8.1. All the rooks are blocked by pawns, but then Black comes up with a plan...

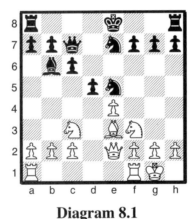

**Diagram 8.1**

Black still needs to castle and develop those rooks.

Black can activate a rook by way of a pawn capture. First, Black plays **1) ...dxe4**, clearing the d-file of pawns. After White recaptures with **2) Nxe4**, Black castles queenside (**O-O-O**). This helps protect the king, and also places a rook on the newly open d-file. White might now try moving a rook onto the open e-file with **Rfe1** (Rae1 would entomb the other rook). Remember that open/closed files refer only to the presence or absence of pawns on those files. It doesn't matter which other pieces are on the file because pieces that are not pawns can vacate the file any time they feel like it. Pawns, on the other hand, must wait for a chance to capture something, or be captured.

## COORDINATION

When pieces work together to help each other, they are said to be **coordinated**. Let's look at a couple of ways in which pieces coordinate with each other to improve your position. One type of coordination is when you have more than one piece attacking a single square. If you attack a piece or a square more times than it is defended, you might win material, or maybe a lot more.

Diagram 8.2 shows White threatening to play the famous four-move checkmate (mentioned in Chapter 4). It works very simply. At the start of the game, White notices that Black's king is the only defender of the f7 square. So f7 is one of Black's weaker squares, just as f2 is weak for White. If White attacks f7 with two pieces (queen and bishop), Black should either block one of those lines of attack, or defend f7 a second time. Otherwise, White will capture on f7. In this position, it's Black to move. The mate on f7 is easily defended with a move like . . . **Qe7**. This not only stops the mate, but also protects Black's e-pawn from being captured by White's queen.

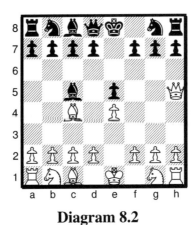

**Diagram 8.2**

White's queen and bishop are coordinated. Black had better do something about the threat of mate on f7. And don't forget the pawn on e5!

Another type of coordination has to do with arranging your pieces so they do not interfere with each other's movement. One example of this idea is the placement of pawns in relation to bishops, as illustrated in Diagram 8.3.

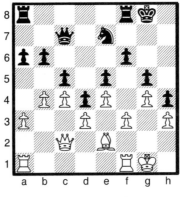

**Diagram 8.3**

White has a bad bishop.

White's bishop on e2 is behaving like a weak pawn right now. It lacks freedom of movement and serves no useful purpose at the moment. It's blocked by its own pawns. Here's a helpful hint for positions where you have only one bishop: Try to keep your pawns, especially center pawns, off the color square occupied by your bishop. This will give your bishop more scope, like the one shown in Diagram 8.4.

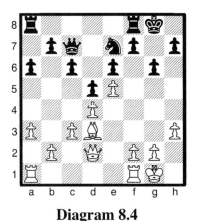

**Diagram 8.4**
White has a good bishop. It guards light squares
while the pawns guard dark squares.

## EXPLOITING WEAKNESSES

In order to gain any kind of advantage in a chess game, your opponent must first have created some kind of weakness in his position. The simplest form of positional weakness is a piece that is **hanging**. This means that someone has carelessly left it where it can be taken for free, or for less than it's worth, as shown in Diagram 8.5.

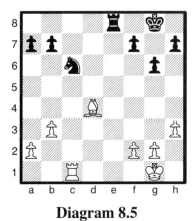

**Diagram 8.5**

It's Black to move. Are any of White's pieces hanging?

White's bishop on d4 is both attacked and undefended. Black can play **...Nxd4**, winning the bishop. A subtler type of weakness is an **under-defended piece**, attacked more strongly than it is defended, as shown in Diagram 8.6.

**Diagram 8.6**

Never underestimate the value of a pawn, especially a center pawn.

Black has endangered his d-pawn. Although it's protected by the bishop on e7, it's attacked twice—by White's bishop on f4 and the queen on d2.

White can play **Bxd6** here, winning a pawn. If Black responds with **...Bxd6**, White goes **Qxd6**. Each player gets a bishop, but White gets an extra pawn. Keep in mind not only the number of attackers and defenders, but also their values. You don't want to take that pawn on d6 with the queen first!

## ATTACKING THE KING

A game is won by checkmating the enemy king. Yet, many beginners develop picces, then play the rest of the game as if expecting the enemy to walk over and surrender. Once you're pieces are developed, you have to aim them toward the enemy king, and the potential escape squares surrounding it. Do this carefully, but without fear. You have nothing to lose but a game of chess. And don't forget to defend your own king when necessary.

If you keep track of king safety throughout the game, you're much more likely to find the winning move once the opportunity presents itself. In the four-move checkmate scenario (Chapter 4), White launches a direct attack against Black's uncastled king by way of the weak f7 square, which Black had better defend, or else. Attack a castled king in the same manner, aiming more than one piece at a single weak square.

Diagram 8.7 shows a position where the kings have castled to opposite sides of the board. When this happens, both sides can advance pawns toward the enemy king, without endangering their own kings.

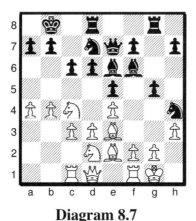

**Diagram 8.7**

The weak (less defended) squares around White's king are
h2 and g2. Around Black's king, a7, b7, and c7.

Aim your pieces at the weak squares surrounding the
enemy king. Or push your pawns toward the enemy's pawns
that shield their king, and try to capture them. A king with no
pawn shield is as vulnerable as a house with no walls.

## DEFENSE

Though everyone likes to attack, the importance of
defensive play is this: your opponent is attacking you too!
Your opponent is trying to exploit your weaknesses. There
are times when you'd better defend yourself before continu-
ing with your attack.

Even experienced players sometimes fall apart when
under attack, but if you study the position calmly, you'll find
many surprising resources that could turn the whole game
around. When under attack, don't give up. Get mad! Fight
back! If you must lose, at least make your opponent work
for the win. Look for ways to save the game, as Black does
in Diagram 8.8.

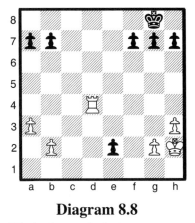

**Diagram 8.8**
Black plays an **in-between** move.

If Black queens the e-pawn now, White will play **Rd8+**, followed by mate next move. So Black defends by playing **...f5** first. This gives the king an escape square (f7), and also prevents White from playing **Re4**, which would attack and capture the e-pawn. Now Black's e-pawn cannot be stopped from queening. Knowing how to play defensively is every bit as important as launching an attack. Offense and defense are two sides of the same coin.

# CHAPTER 8: REVIEW QUESTIONS

**1.** What is a minor piece?

**2.** What is the middle game?

**3.** What is an open file?

**4.** What is a half-open file?

**5.** Why do rooks like open files?

**6.** How do you open a file?

**7.** What is coordination?

**8.** If you have a dark squared bishop, but your other bishop is gone, on what color squares do you want your center pawns?

**9.** What does it mean for a piece to be hanging?

**10.** How can pawns assist your attack?

# 9. ENDGAME STRATEGY

The **endgame** is the final stage of a chess game, when most pieces have been traded off, and all that remain are kings, one or more pawns, and sometimes one or two other pieces. Although there are very few fighters left on the board, the endgame is not always easy to play, and sometimes requires great precision to win, or even to draw. In this chapter we discuss three very important endgame themes:

**1.** The king as a fighting piece

**2.** The opposition

**3.** Creating a passed pawn.

## THE KING AS A FIGHTING PIECE

Until the endgame, keeping the king safe from attack is of great importance. But once most of the forces have been traded away, especially queens, the king is in much less danger of getting checkmated. So it is now free to advance, attack pawns or other pieces, and face the other king. Diagram 9.1 shows that White's king, having marched toward the center, is about to eat up all of Black's pawns (starting with the undefended one on c7), while Black's king crouches uselessly in a corner. White will play **Kxc7**, followed by **Kxd6**, then will most likely queen the d-pawn and win the game. Black could have at least drawn the game if his king had been nearby enough to attack White's pawns or defend his own pawns.

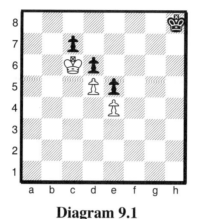

**Diagram 9.1**

White is a pawn behind, but will soon he a queen ahead,
thanks to a well-placed king.

## OPPOSITION

In the endgame, a king wants to advance, whether to attack or to defend. The position shown in Diagram 9.2 is a draw by insufficient mating material, but it can be useful in making a point about advancing kings. Let's say, in this position, both kings want to advance as soon as possible. Pretend that the first king to advance (move forward one rank) wins the game. Suppose it's White's move. White cannot advance, since doing so would put his king in check. Unfortunately, White has to move somewhere. So the white king must either retreat or step aside.

Either way, the black king will then be able to advance. For example, if White plays **Ke3**, Black can play **Kc4**, advancing. If instead White plays **Kc3**, Black can still advance with **Ke4**. Often in king and pawn endgames, when the kings are facing (opposing) each other directly, you want it to be your opponent's move, because whoever has to move must step out of the way, allowing the other king to advance. Whoever does not have to move has the advantage of being the first player able to advance, and this type of advantage is called the **opposition**. In Diagram 9.2, since it's White's move, Black has the opposition.

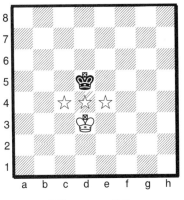

**Diagram 9.2**
Squares attacked by both kings are marked with stars.

Opposition is most clearly illustrated when all that is left on the board are kings and just one pawn. The pawn would like to become a queen, but in order to avoid being captured by the enemy king, its own king has to advance along with it for protection. The player with the extra pawn uses the opposition to force that pawn safely to a queening square, with mate soon to follow. The player with the lone king uses the opposition to stop the enemy pawn from queening, in order to draw a game that otherwise would have been lost.

To see how the opposition works in an actual game, take a look at Diagram 9.3. It's White to move. White has six possible moves here. Five of them will tie the game, and only one will win! Can you find the winning move for White? Here's a hint: White has to take the opposition.

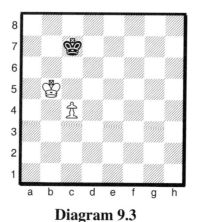

**Diagram 9.3**
Here, White's strongest weapon
(and Black's best defense) is the opposition!

If you suggested **Kc5** for White, you are correct. **Kc5** is the only move that sets up a situation where the kings face (oppose) each other when it is Black's turn to move. **Kc5** forces Black to step to one side or retreat, so the White king can advance to b6, c6, or d6. After **Kc5**, White can't be stopped. The game could continue like this, starting from Diagram 9.3:

|  | **White** | **Black** |
|---|---|---|
| **1** | **Kc5** |  |

Seizing the opposition.

|  | | |
|---|---|---|
| **1** | **...** | **Kb7** |
| **2** | **Kd6** | |

Advancing.

|  | | |
|---|---|---|
| **2** | **...** | **Kc8** |
| **3** | **Kc6** | |

Keeping the opposition.

| 3 | ... | Kb8 |
|---|---|---|
| 4 | Kd7 | |

To protect the pawn as it promotes.

| 4 | ... | Kb7 |
|---|---|---|
| 5 | c5 | |

This pawn cannot be stopped.

| 5 | ... | Kb8 |
|---|---|---|
| 6 | c6 | Ka7 |
| 7 | c7 | Kb7 |
| 8 | c8=Q+ | |

...and White will soon mate with queen and king vs. king, using the technique shown in Chapter 6.

What if White had played, say, **c5** instead of **Kc5**? Pushing the pawn at that time would have allowed Black to play **Kb7**, grabbing the opposition. Then the game might have gone like this, starting from Diagram 9.3:

| 1 | c5 | Kb7! |
|---|---|---|

(takes the opposition)

| 2 | c6+ | Kc7 |
|---|---|---|

(blocks the pawn)

| 3 | Kc5 | Kc8 |
|---|---|---|

(keeps the opposition)

| 4 | Kd6 | Kd8 |
|---|---|---|
| 5 | c7+ | Kc8 |
| 6 | Kc6 | |

...and Black is stalemated! The game is drawn, because Black took the opposition after White let it get away. When a lone king takes the opposition, it will often be able to draw, either by getting itself stalemated or by capturing the enemy pawn. By the way, if the extra pawn is an a-pawn or an h-pawn, the game will be drawn no matter who has the opposition, provided that the lone king can get in front of the enemy pawn.

## PASSED PAWNS

A **passed pawn** is a pawn that cannot be stopped from queening (i.e. cannot be blocked or captured) by enemy pawns. Which pawns shown in Diagram 9.4 are passed pawns? Keep in mind that whether or not a pawn is passed depends only on the positioning of the opponent's pawns.

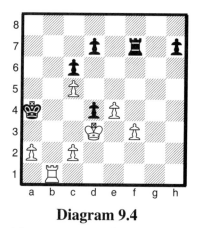

**Diagram 9.4**

White's a- and f-pawns are passed, and so is Black's h-pawn.

In Diagram 9.5, it's White's move. White can create a passed pawn by playing **c5**! Now the white c-pawn cannot be stopped by other pawns from queening. If White had instead played **cxd5**, Black could have played **exd5**, leaving the opposing d-pawns blocked. White's b-pawn and Black's a-pawn are not passed, since either pawn could capture the other pawn as they approach one another.

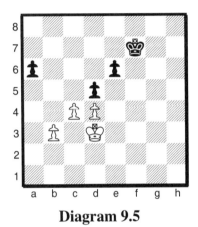

**Diagram 9.5**

Create a "passer" if possible. A passed pawn has a
much better chance of becoming a queen.

When you have more pawns on one side of the board than your opponent does, you have what's called a kingside or queenside **pawn majority**. Often, you can use this majority to create a passed pawn. In Diagram 9.6, White has three pawns on the queenside, and Black has only two. So White has a queenside pawn majority.

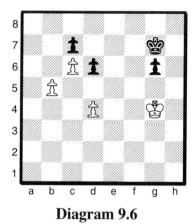

**Diagram 9.6**

Black's king is too far away to help fight White's extra queenside pawn.

White can force a passed pawn by playing **b6**! If Black then plays **cxb6**, White will play **c7**, followed by **c8=Q**. If Black doesn't take on b6, then White can just play **b7**, followed by **b8=Q**.

Diagram 9.7 shows an unusual scenario in which the kingside pawns are equal, with Black to move, but Black creates a passer anyway. Can you see how?

**Diagram 9.7**

Both sides will end up with passed pawns, but Black will queen first.

**1) ...g3** creates the passer. If White plays **2) ...f3**, Black goes **2) ...gxh2**. If White plays **2) h3**, then Black will play **2) ...gxf2**. Even if White tries a move like **2) ...fxg3**, Black will reply with **2) . .h3**, threatening **3) ...hxg2**. If White tries to defend with **3) gxh3**, Black will play **3) ...f3**, followed by **4) ...f2**, and **5) ...f1=Q**.

## 9. REVIEW QUESTIONS:

**1.** What is the endgame?

**2.** How does the role of a king change in the endgame?

**3.** What is the opposition?

**4.** What do you do with the opposition when you have a lone king and your opponent has a king and pawn?

**5.** What do you do with the opposition when you have a king and pawn and your opponent has a lone king?

**6.** If you have a king and pawn and your opponent has just a king, but keeps the opposition, what will most likely be the result of the game?

**7.** What is a passed pawn?

**8.** What's good about a passed pawn?

**9.** What is a king side pawn majority?

**10.** What can you sometimes do with a pawn majority?

# 10. THE MIGHTY PAWN

Much of what we learn in this chapter is mentioned in other places throughout the book. But so many beginners underestimate the value of a pawn that the subject deserves special attention.

The pawn, as you now know, is the least valuable of the chess pieces, mainly because of its restricted mobility. A pawn makes small moves, and cannot retreat. It lacks the scope of other pieces. But remember that a pawn can serve all of the following functions:

1. **A pawn can not only make captures**, a pawn often gives itself up for a more valuable piece. Consider White's d-pawn in Diagram 10.1.

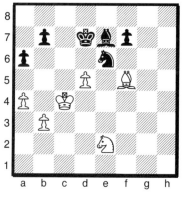

**Diagram 10.1**
White can win material, or make an even trade.

If White plays **Bxe6+**, Black can play **...fxe6**, and White has traded a bishop for a knight. But White can instead play **dxe6+**. This also captures the knight, but Black only gets a pawn for it with **...fxe6**. Then White's attacked bishop can simply move to a safer square.

### 2. A pawn can defend a bigger piece.

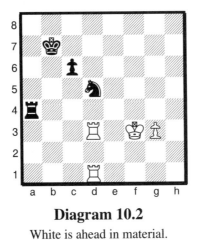

**Diagram 10.2**

White is ahead in material.

White would not want to play **Rxd5** here, because after Black responds with **...cxd5**, and White answers **Rxd5**, White has given up a rook (worth 5) for a knight and pawn (worth 4). But imagine a black bishop on c6 instead of a black pawn. Then White probably should play **Rxd5**. When Black replies with **...Bxd5**, White can play **Rxd5** with the remaining rook. White would end up with a bishop and a knight (6), for the rook (5). Thanks to the defensive powers of the pawn on c6, Black's knight is immune from capture at this time.

### 3. Pawns can defend each other.

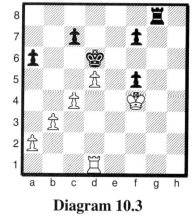

**Diagram 10.3**

White's pawns are **connected**. Black's pawns are **isolated**.

White's d5 pawn is defended by the c4 pawn, which is defended by the b3 pawn, which is defended by the a2 pawn. A string of pawns defending each other in this way is called a **pawn chain**. The undefended pawn at the back (in this case, the one on a2) is called the **base** of the pawn chain, and this is the weak spot Black wants to attack (perhaps with a move like **...Rg2**). Black's pawns cannot defend one another, so they're more susceptible to attack. For instance, how will Black defend the pawn on f5?

### 4. Pawns can perform tactical maneuvers.

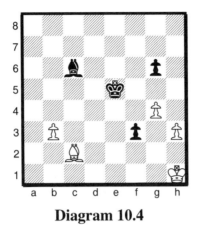

**Diagram 10.4**
With Black to move, the f-pawn is deadly.

Here, Black wins by a **discovered check** with **...f2+**, followed by **...f1=Q**. White is powerless to stop the slaughter. In addition to discoveries, pawns can also execute *forks*, as well as participating in more advanced tactics such as *clearance, interference, deflection, in-between moves*, and *removing the guard* (see glossary).

### 5. Pawns can give check (and even checkmate!)

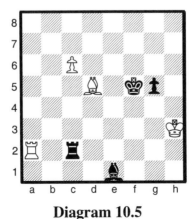

**Diagram 10.5**
Who's afraid of the big, bad pawn? White. That's who.

Can you find the checkmate here for Black? If you found all the checks, I guarantee you've found the checkmate. Right! Black can play **...g4++**.

6. **Pawns control squares.** So, a pawn can be used to gain space for your other pieces, and to chase your opponent's pieces away.

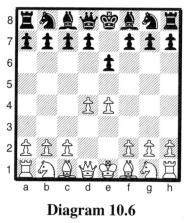

**Diagram 10.6**

White has a spatial advantage.

Here, White's pawns control four squares in Black's territory, namely c5, d5, e5, and f5. Black's bigger pieces cannot occupy those squares for now. So far, the game has gone **1) e4; e6 2) d4**. If Black now plays, say, **2) ...Nf6**, White can chase the knight by playing **3) e5**. If instead Black tries **2)...Bb4+**, White can "kick" the bishop with **3) c3**. Pawns can be such a nuisance.

7. **Pawns can form a shield to protect your king from enemy forces.**

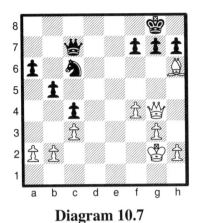

**Diagram 10.7**

If not for the pawn shield, Black's king would already be in check,
with mate soon to follow!

In this position, Black's g-pawn is **pinned**, and therefore
can't take the bishop. White is threatening **Qxg7++**. But
Black can utilize that pawn shield with a move like **...g6,**
defending the g-pawn with the f- and h-pawns.

### 8. Pawns can promote.

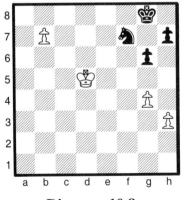

**Diagram 10.8**

Which would YOU rather have, White's vicious b-pawn
or Black's harmless knight?

# PAWN STRUCTURE

Pawn structure is the formation (placement) of pawns in relation to each other. The following diagrams show various elements of pawn structure:

**Diagram 10.9**

A fixed (blockaded) pawn structure. Opposing pawns prevent each other from moving.

**Diagram 10.10**

A fluid (dynamic) pawn structure. These pawns have options.

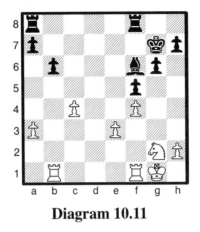

**Diagram 10.11**

White has a broken pawn structure. These pawns are weak and subject to attack. Black has a clear advantage.

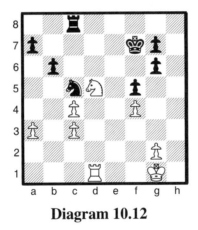

**Diagram 10.12**

Black's pawns are **doubled** on the g-file. White's pawns on the c-file are doubled and isolated.

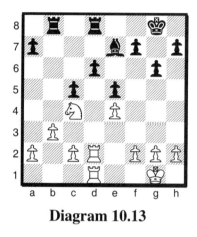

**Diagram 10.13**

Black has a backward d-pawn. Its would-be defenders, the c- and e-pawns, are too far advanced to protect it. This pawn is vulnerable to attack, as it can't be defended by another pawn. The square in front of a **backward** pawn is called a **hole** in the position, and your pieces can often park themselves there, since they can't be chased away by enemy pawns. Black has a hole on d5.

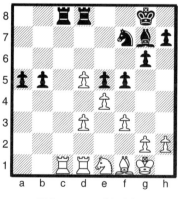

**Diagram 10.14**

Black has connected passed pawns on the a- and b-files. They support each other's advance, and control the squares in front of them. White has a passed pawn on d5.

## CHAPTER 10: REVIEW QUESTIONS

Answers to some of these questions may appear in Chapters 1 & 3, or in the glossary at the end of this book.

1. What can a pawn do that no other piece can do?
2. Why is a pawn considered the least valuable piece?
3. What is pawn structure?
4. What is a blockaded pawn structure?
5. What are doubled pawns?
6. What is an isolated pawn?
7. What is a backward pawn?
8. What is a pawn chain?
9. What is a pawn storm?
1o. What tactics can a pawn perform?

# 11. BASIC TACTICS

**Tactics** are the tricks your pieces can do to win other pieces or to improve your position in some way. The simplest tactical form is one we have already seen, known as the **single threat**—one piece threatening to capture one other piece. In Diagram 11.1, White's knight is threatened by Black's pawn on c5. Leaving the knight hanging there would be a tactical mistake in this example, so White ought to move the knight. But **Nf3** would also be a tactical mistake. Can you see why? Hint: What pieces are attacking what other pieces? What pieces are defending those attacked pieces? Try looking two or three moves ahead. You may be surprised to find that this is not as hard as you thought it would be.

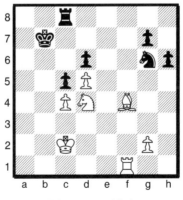

**Diagram 11.1**

Even simple looking positions like this one are loaded
with tricks and traps called tactics.

If you looked carefully, you saw that Black's knight on g6 attacks the white bishop on f4, although the white rook on f1 defends it. No problem here, unless White plays **Nf3** now. This blocks the rook's defense, so it can no longer protect the bishop. Then Black can play **...Nxf4**, winning the bishop. Even if you failed to see the details, **Nf3** seems intuitively wrong just by virtue of not being an attacking move. A better move for White than **Nf3** would be **Nb5**, threatening **Nxd6+**, which would attack Black's king and rook simultaneously.

The next tactical level is called the **double (or multiple) threat**—a move that makes two or more threats at once. One example of a double threat is the **fork**—when one piece threatens two or more pieces at the same time. Any piece, even the king, can fork two other pieces. Forks are dangerous, and can be difficult to defend. Often, when two pieces are forked, one of them will be lost. The following six diagrams show different kinds of forks.

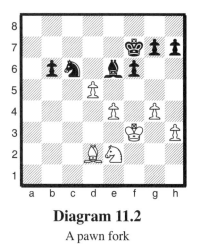

**Diagram 11.2**
A pawn fork

In Diagram 11.2 White has just played **d5**, so the d-pawn is forking Black's knight and bishop. In some positions,

Black would be forced to lose either the knight or the bishop. But Black, refusing to accept defeat, finds a clever defensive resource. **1) ...Ne5+** does two things: it gets the knight away from the threatening pawn and puts the white king in check. White has to use this move to get out of check. After that, it's Black's move again, and he can now retreat the bishop to d7 or c8, avoiding capture. Then Black will have successfully defended this pawn fork.

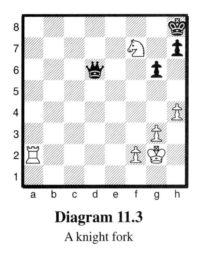

**Diagram 11.3**
A knight fork

In Diagram 11.3, White has just played a murderous knight fork. **Nf7+** threatens Black's queen and checks the king. When Black gets out of check, as he must, White's knight will capture the black queen. After that, White should win easily with all those extra pieces. Black has no defense to this fork.

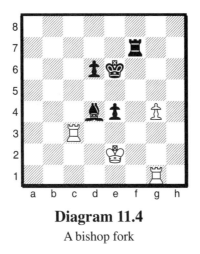

**Diagram 11.4**
A bishop fork

In Diagram 11.4 the black bishop forks the rook on c3 and the rook on g1. White looks for a rook check or some larger threat, but does not find one. The best White can do is protect one rook with the other rook by playing, for example, **Rgcl**. White still has to give up a rook and only get a bishop in return. This is known as **losing the exchange**, but it's better than losing a rook for nothing.

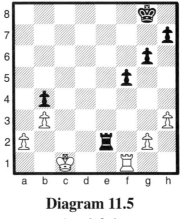

**Diagram 11.5**
A rook fork

A rook on its own 7th rank can be powerful, as shown in Diagram 11.5. It can trap the king to an edge, and often attacks more than one pawn at a time. This rook forks White's a- and g-pawns. One of them will fall next move.

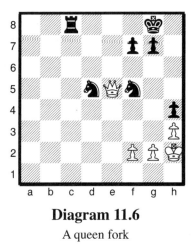

**Diagram 11.6**
A queen fork

The queen in Diagram 11.6 forks the Black knights. A good defensive move for Black is **...Nde7** or **...Nfe7**, so the knights defend each other.

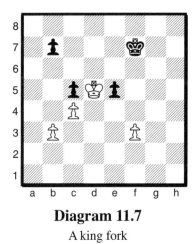

**Diagram 11.7**
A king fork

White's king is forking Black's c- and e-pawns. Black can protect one or the other, but not both of them. White should win eventually.

Another type of double threat involves a **discovered check**. This happens when one piece moves out of the way of another friendly piece, so that the other piece checks the enemy king. In Diagram 11.8 it's White to move. If White moves the bishop *anywhere*, the black king will be in check by White's rook on f1. Any bishop move results in a discovered check by White's rook. No matter where the bishop goes, Black will have to use his/her move to get out of check. So White makes a double threat by playing **Be4+!** This move not only attacks Black's king with the rook, but at the same time attacks Black's queen with the bishop! Black has no way to meet both threats at once, and must get out of check. Then, White will play **Bxa8**, winning the queen.

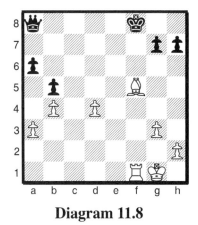

**Diagram 11.8**

A discovered check is best when played in conjunction with another threat.

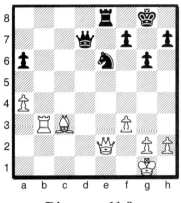

**Diagram 11.9**

A discovered attack doesn't have to be check.

Here, Black can play **...Nc5**, which attacks White's rook with the knight while also attacking White's queen with the rook on e8. White loses material to this discovery.

A very common tactic is the **pin**. An attacked piece is pinned when it cannot (or should not) move because doing so would endanger the piece behind it. In Diagram 11.10, White's bishop is pinned against its own king. It can't move without exposing its own king to check, by the rook on e8.

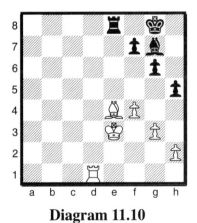

**Diagram 11.10**

If it's Black's move, ...f5 wins the pinned bishop, since it cannot move. If it's White to move, Kf3 is recommended to "break "the pin, while still defending the bishop.

Black's knight in Diagram 11.11 is pinned against its own queen by White's bishop on g2. If the black knight moves, White's bishop will take the queen. White can exploit this pin by playing **Ne5**, doubly attacking Black's paralyzed knight, which cannot be doubly defended, and will be captured next move.

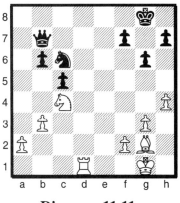

**Diagram 11.11**

Either Rd6 or Ne5 puts Black's pinned knight under double attack.

Another kind of tactic is a **skewer**. This occurs when two pieces are in the same line of attack, though only one of them is threatened at the moment. In Diagram 11.12, Black's bishop is skewering White's two rooks. In other words, when one rook moves away, the other rook remains exposed to the bishop's attack. The skewer gets its name from its resemblance to a shish kebab. In this case, the bishop represents the pointed metal kitchen utensil known as a skewer, while White's rooks suggest chunks of meat impaled on it.

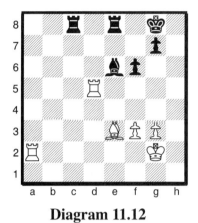

**Diagram 11.12**

White has left both rooks on the same line of attack.
They can't both be saved.

Diagram 11.13 shows two knights being skewered by a rook.

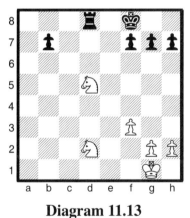

**Diagram 11.13**

White has left both knights on the same line of attack.
Black's rook will feast on one of them next move.

# CHAPTER 11: REVIEW QUESTIONS

**1.** What is a tactic?

**2.** What is a fork?

**3.** What types of pieces can fork other pieces?

**4.** What is a discovery?

**5.** What is a pin?

**6.** How do you take advantage of a pin?

**7.** What is a skewer?

**8.** What is a double threat?

**9.** Can a knight skewer two pieces?

**10.** How do you take advantage of a discovery?

# 12. SEEING THE FUTURE—THE ART OF COMBINATIONS

A **combination** is any sequence of moves that forces some kind of improvement in your position. This improvement could mean controlling more squares, winning material, queening a pawn, or even a sure fire mating attack. Three unique features of a combination are 1) it's forced, so there is nothing your opponent can do to stop it, 2) it usually includes a tactic, and 3) it often involves a **sacrifice**. In chess, sacrifice generally means to give up material in return for something more valuable. In Diagram 12.1, it's White to move. White remembers the crucial principle, always look for checks, and after examining what would happen next, plays a stunning combination.

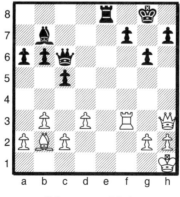

**Diagram 12.1**

Black threatens to play ...Re1+, with mate to follow.
But White's queen, rook, and bishop have lots of scope.

If you're always looking for checks, by now you've noticed **1) Qxh7+**. At first glance, this seems like an awful move because Black can play **1) ...Kxh7**, capturing the queen! In fact, Black is forced to take the queen, because if he plays his only other legal move, **1) ...Kf8**, White will play **2) Qxf7++** (the white queen would be defended by the rook on f3).

White has now sacrificed a whole queen, but is very soon rewarded for his bravery. The game continued like this (starting from Diagram 12.1):

| | White | Black |
|---|---|---|
| 1 | Qxh7+ | |

A queen sacrifice.

| | | |
|---|---|---|
| 1 | ... | Kxh7 |
| 2 | Rh3+ | Kg8 |

Black's only legal move.

| | | |
|---|---|---|
| 3 | Rh8++ | |

White's rook is defended by the b2 bishop.

Although material was even in the above position, White won quickly by having placed pieces on squares where they'd be most active, and therefore most likely to allow a winning combination. Black had some dangerous threats too, but it's awfully hard to carry out an attack when your king is in check.

The position in Diagram 12.2 shows Black ahead in material, a piece count of 23 vs. 21. By comparison, Black has a rook vs. White's knight with White to move. But White, always on the lookout for checks, sacrifices the knight with a very forcing move.

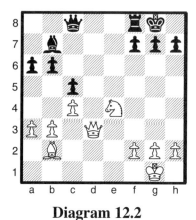

**Diagram 12.2**

White's queen, bishop and knight all seem to AIM toward Black's king,
don't they? Black's queen and rook, on the other hand,
are not as conveniently placed.

This game ended with White playing the following combination:

|   | White | Black |
|---|-------|-------|
| 1 | Nf6+  | gxf6  |

If Black had played ...Kh8, then Qxh7 would be mate.

|   | White | Black |
|---|-------|-------|
| 2 | Qg3+  | Kh8   |

2...Qg4 could have prevented mate for one more move.

|   | White  |
|---|--------|
| 3 | Bxf6++ |

In Diagram 12.3, the game is only four and a half moves
old, but Black notices that White has overextended his
pieces a bit. In other words, White's undefended knight and
bishop have wandered into Black's territory, so they may be
susceptible to attack. Also, White has not yet castled, and the
white king stands on open lines. Noticing these weaknesses

in White's position, Black seeks and finds a combination that wins the knight.

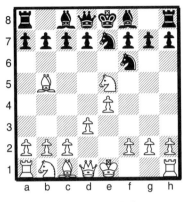

**Diagram 12.3**

If you notice a weakness in your opponent's position,
look for a combination.

|  | **White** | **Black** |
|---|---|---|
| 1 | ... | c6 |

Attacks the bishop and opens a line for Black's queen.

|  | White | Black |
|---|---|---|
| 2 | Bc4 | Qa5+ |

A queen fork! Attacks White's king and knight.

|  | White | Black |
|---|---|---|
| 3 | Bd2 | Qxe5 |

Black should be able to win this game eventually, as an experienced player can win most games when ahead by a knight or more. Diagram 12.4 shows a position where Black pulls off a winning combination due to an **overworked piece**. See, White's rook is busy defending the bishop on g3 and the pawn on f4. Black finds a way to take advantage of this weakness:

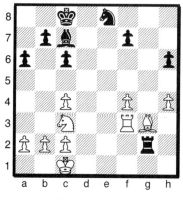

**Diagram 12.4**

An overworked piece dies from exhaustion.

|  | White | Black |
|---|---|---|
| 1 | ... | Rxg3 |

Sacs the rook for a bishop, but only for a moment.

|  | White | Black |
|---|---|---|
| 2 | Rxg3 | Bxf4+ |

A bishop fork! Attacks White's king and rook.

Now, no matter what White does to get out of check, Black's bishop will take White's rook next move, so Black wins a bishop and a pawn in that transaction.

Diagram 12.5 shows a position where White plays a combination that uses a tactic called **deflection**. This means coaxing a piece away from where it needs to be. In this case, White wants to queen the a-pawn, but if a7 now, Black could play **...Kb7**, capturing the pawn next move, and drawing the game. So White gets an idea...

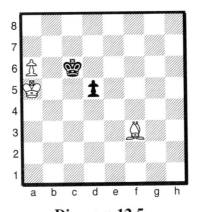

**Diagram 12.5**

Wouldn't it be nice for White if Black's king were
further away from the a-pawn?

| | White | Black |
|---|---|---|
| 1 | Bxd5+ | Kxd5 |

Black has no better move.

| | White | Black |
|---|---|---|
| 2 | a7 | Kc6 |

Can't get back to the pawn in time.

| | White | |
|---|---|---|
| 3 | a8=Q | |

...and White will win with queen and king vs. king.

As you can see, there are many different types of combinations. The best way to find a combination is just to put
your pieces on open lines, slowly strengthening your position, and keep looking. Expect to miscalculate and lose the
game sometimes. This is a normal part of practicing chess.
You'll eventually start to find brilliant combinations as long
as you remember to:

**1.** Develop your pieces to useful squares.

**2.** Attack the center with pieces and pawns.

**3.** Notice weaknesses in your opponent's position.

**4.** Look for threats, especially checks!

**5.** Look for tactics (forks, pins, skewers, etc.).

See if you can find the winning combination in each of the following five positions from actual tournament games. Each diagram tells you whose move it is. Solving puzzles like these is a good way to sharpen your combinational skills. Don't worry about whether or not you get them right. There are thousands more where these came from. This is not a test, but simply an illustration of the miracles that take place on a chessboard. Combinations are the heart of chess. See for yourself and be amazed! Answers with explanations appear at the end of this chapter.

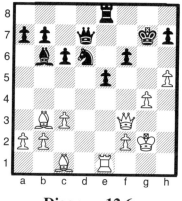

**Diagram 12.6**
White to play and win (tactic: deflection).

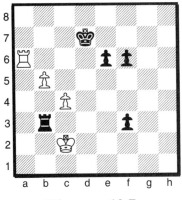

**Diagram 12.7**

Black to play and win (tactic: interference).

**Diagram 12.8**

White to play and win (tactic: double check).

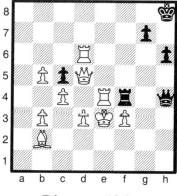

**Diagram 12.9**

Black to play and draw (tactic: counterattack).

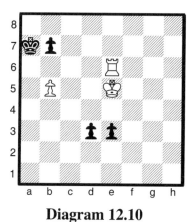

**Diagram 12.10**

White to play and win (tactic: unclassified).

## ANSWERS

### Diagram 12.6: Deflection

1    Bh6+         Kh8

(if Black plays 1) ...Kxh6, then 2) Qxf6 is mate)

2    Qxf6+       Qg7

(Black's only move)

3    Qxg7++

White offers a bishop (though Black doesn't take it) in order to drive Black's king away from the pawn it had been guarding on f6.

### Diagram 12.7: Interference

1                  ...Rb1

(White threatened Ra1, stopping the f-pawn)

2    Kxb1         f2

Black runs interference by sacrificing a rook, forcing White's king to get in the way of his own rook. Now Black cannot be stopped from queening the f-pawn. Black gives up a rook, but gets back a queen!

### Diagram 12.8: Double check

1    Qd8+ (a queen sac!)      Kxd8 (forced)

2    Ba5+ (double check)      Kc8 (or Ke8)

3    Rd8++

When a king is double checked (this can only happen by way of a discovered check), it must move, since you can't block or capture two pieces at once.

## Diagram 12.9: Counterattack

| 1 | ... | Qe1+ |
|---|---|---|
| 2 | Kxf4 | Qh4+ |
| 3 | Kf5 (or Ke5) | Qh5+ |
| 4 | Ke6 | Qe8+ |
| 5 | Kf5 | Qh5+ |

Black was behind in material by a rook, a bishop, and two pawns. This adds up to more than the value of a queen! Black needed, and found, a defensive combination that resulted in a draw by perpetual check. It's a good thing Black remembered to look for checks.

## Diagram 12.10: Unclassified

White has no way of stopping Black's d- or e-pawn from queening. But White, ever the fighter, searches for a miracle, and finds one. With a rare stroke of genius, White lets Black have the queen, then gives up a rook, and mates in a few moves anyway.

| 1 | Kd6 | d2 |
|---|---|---|
| 2 | Kc7 | d1=Q |

(Black will never move this queen)

| 3 | Ra6+ | bxa6 |
|---|---|---|

(this, and Black's remaining moves, are forced)

| 4 | b6+ | Ka8 |
|---|---|---|
| 5 | b7+ | Ka7 |
| 6 | b8=Q++ | |

Surprises like these are why people love chess.

## CHAPTER 12: REVIEW QUESTIONS:

**1.** What is a combination?

**2.** What is a sacrifice?

**3.** When should a player look for checks?

**4.** When should a player look for a combination?

**5.** What is an overworked piece?

**6.** What is deflection?

**7.** What is interference?

**8.** What is double check?

**9.** How is double check possible?

**10.** What is a countcrattack?

# 13. THE TEN MOST COMMON BEGINNER'S MISTAKES

This section outlines strategic errors frequently made by beginners of all ages. Most chess players correct these problems eventually, but reading this chapter will help you avoid them altogether.

## 1. Counting captured forces

New players often find it more convenient to count captured pieces, especially when most pieces are still in play. However, this is a very bad habit. Captured pieces are of no importance to the game in progress, and counting them will only draw your attention away from your position. Count only the pieces on the board, even if it's harder to do. Developing good playing habits will improve your game, even if you never study chess on a serious level.

## 2. Copying your opponent's moves

For some reason, beginners often see this as a viable strategic option. But copying your opponent's moves just for the sake of copying moves makes no sense at all. Imagine the following moves:

| 1 | e4 | e5 |

So far, so good.

| 2 | Qh5 | Qh4 |
|---|-----|-----|

Oops.

| 3 | Qxh4 | ... |
|---|------|-----|

Black will have a problem copying that one.

## 3. Ignoring your opponent's last move

Many beginners seem to forget they have an opponent, going about their plans without noticing the plans being made against them. This type of oversight is most commonly seen in forgetting to recapture. It's important that you ask yourself on every turn, "What was my opponent's last move? Why did he play that move? What, if anything, does it do? What, if anything, should I do about it?"

## 4. Counting on your opponent's mistakes

New players will frequently play a move that's advantageous only if the opponent makes a specific error. This practice is generally unsound. What are the chances your opponent will play exactly the moves you want? And if your opponent responds correctly, you've weakened your position or, at least, wasted time. Ideally, each move you make should improve your position no matter what your opponent does. However, there are exceptions. For instance, your game may already be hopelessly lost. It can't hurt to damage your position further if you were completely lost anyway. There are times when giving your opponent a chance to screw up is your last opportunity to save the game. So in some cases, an inferior move is actually the best try!

## 5. Fear of ghosts

This refers to avoiding a move because "something might happen." An example of this occurs in the way many beginners like to save their most powerful pieces for later. That's like being involved in a shootout and saving your gun for later. Go ahead and move your queen out! Just be sure to look before you leap. The entire board is always visible to both players. Your opponent cannot hide anything from you. The best thing you can do for yourself as a chess player is to play carefully, but without fear.

## 6. Flank rook development

Beginners often develop their rooks in the way shown in Diagram 13.1, where White has played **1) h4**, then **2) Rh3**. Rooks developed this way can be captured by enemy bishops. All the opponent has to do is move a center pawn to open a line for the attacking bishop. Proper rook development takes a little longer, as we saw in Chapter 8.

**Diagram 13.1**
Black, to move, can play ...Bxh3.

## 7. Checking just because you can

As mentioned earlier, it's important to examine all the available checks in a position. However, check is not always the best move. A simple illustration of this point can be seen in Diagram 13.2. White has just played **3) Bb5+**. Developing the bishop is not a bad idea, but Black can reply **3) ...c6**, chasing the bishop away. That bishop would have been better off on c4.

**Diagram 13.2**

This check is all bark and no bite.

## 8. Moving the king when in check

Running away when under attack seems to be the first impulse for many new players who find themselves in check. But if you haven't castled yet, moving the king should generally be considered the last of your three options for escaping check (Chapter 1). In Diagram 13.2, Black could play **3) ...Ke7**. But doing so would forfeit castling privileges, and slow the development of Black's dark squared bishop.

## 9. Ignoring the king's attacking potential

Beginners frequently tend to overlook king captures. Maybe it's because we've all been taught that a king has to be defended. But it's important to remember that a king can advance, attack, capture pieces, and control squares, especially in the endgame.

## 10. Blindly following principles

This happens all the time. Because chess is so complex, it's tempting to lean on general ideas that work much of the time. But don't get carried away. Principles are useful guidelines to assist you when you're short on ideas. But principles are designed to be broken. It's usually okay, for instance, to postpone your opening development for a move or two if you can win material. It's also okay to sacrifice material for an attack that will lead to checkmate.

# 14. CHESS PSYCHOLOGY

Here's where we discuss mental habits that can help you play better chess regardless of experience, talent, or skill level. This section is not about misleading or distracting your opponent. I do not advocate bad sportsmanship, though some players go to great lengths to intimidate their opponents. Grandmaster Najdorf once smacked himself audibly in the forehead, hoping to cause his opponent to mistake a piece sacrifice for a blunder. This works charmingly at times, but betrays a pathetic lack of class in the person doing it. On the other hand, Bobby Fischer, perhaps the greatest chess player of all time, was once asked what he did to psych out his opponents. He said, "I play good moves." Now that's chess psychology. The following tips will help you play good moves more often.

## 1. Relax

In other words, set your ego aside for now. Ignore all previous mistakes and losses, and ignore what you imagine are the opinions of others. Do spectators make you nervous? If so, you're probably concerned that you'll make bad moves and they'll think you're an idiot. Maybe this will help: you don't know what other people really think of you, and you're not likely to find out. So you might as well stop worrying about it. The world is your chessboard. Live entirely in the moment of each position.

## 2. Focus

This is difficult to achieve at first, but so is anything worthwhile. Playing chess is a great way to improve your focus, simply because the nature of the game requires you to exercise that ability. One way to maintain your concentration is to stay seated unless you have a very good reason for getting up. Very good reasons include necessary trips to the restroom and the building being on fire. Think on your opponent's time as well as your own, and try not to talk to anyone during your game. Stuff cotton (or your fingers) in your ears to block out extraneous noises if they're bothering you. If you're feeling somewhat tired or not entirely alert, splash cold water in your face (this can be considered a necessary trip to the restroom). Focus is further improved by a reasonably healthy diet, enough sleep, and moderate exercise.

## 3. Be thorough

Unless your next move is absolutely forced, you should always consider candidate moves. Examine all reasonable options. Avoid impulsive behavior and snap judgements. A single hasty move can lose a game you spent hours trying to win. No matter how definite your plan, check your calculations on every move. Take your time.

## 4. Think positively

There's nothing your opponent can do that you can't see or understand. The entire position is visible to both players at all times. Try to think in terms of what's good about your position, or what you might do to improve it. Play fearlessly. Losing is not synonymous with failure. On the contrary, losing is a natural part of the process of becoming a stronger player. Some of my best friends are losers.

## 5. Avoid personal judgements

Never underestimate or overestimate your opponent or yourself. Personal value judgements are useless at best. Thoughts like "I'm losing" or "No way I could beat a master" are self-fulfilling prophecies. Even seemingly positive thoughts like "I'm winning" can lead to overconfident behavior, which can lead to disaster. Abandon irrelevant, self-imposed limitations on yourself and others. For now, imagine your opponent as nothing more (and nothing less) than the opposite color army. Evaluate each position as if it were a diagram printed on a page, and simply find the best move under the circumstances.

## 6. Avoid manipulative behavior

One example of this is trying to trick the opponent with body language. This is common practice among some chess players, but for several reasons I don't personally recommend it. First, it's unprofessional and makes you look like a con artist. Second, any time spent trying to psych out your opponent is time not spent focusing on your position. Third, if anyone cares, it's just plain dishonest, and not in keeping with the spirit of good chess.

Another commonly seen manipulation technique you'll want to avoid is blitzing (playing super fast) on your opponent's time pressure. Not a good idea. Moving fast when your opponent is short on time only increases the likelihood that you will blunder.

## 7. Avoid generalization

It's often been said that there are more possible chess games than there are electrons in the universe. So it's necessary for you to follow basic principles, and to rely heavily on our intuition when selecting moves. Every position has specific qualities truly unique to that position so give it the proper attention and keep an open mind. Resist preconceived notions. Beware of those ragged cliches (also known as principles) such as "Don't move your queen out early," "Develop knights before bishops," "Don't weaken your pawn structure," and "Move your pieces toward the center." These are only *guidelines*. If you rely on them, they'll betray you.

Ask yourself at every turn, "What's going on in this particular position? All things considered, what really *is* the best move here?"

## 8. Reveal nothing

This refers to acting as if you know what you're doing at all times. For instance, if you realize you've blundered just as you reach to press your clock, follow through with the motion like everything's perfectly normal. Don't wince, flinch, or hesitate. Don't start shaking your knee under the table, unless you were *already* doing so, in which case don't stop. Avoid eye contact with anyone. Try not to blush; don't reveal anything that may tip off an opponent to a blunder.

## 9. Play the most annoying move

When several moves look equally good to you, play the one that makes the biggest threat. If no direct threats exist, play the move that leaves your opponent's pieces the most awkwardly placed, or perhaps the move that takes up the most space in your opponent's territory. If your opponent is in time trouble (but you're not) and several moves look equally good to you, play the move that leads to the most complications. This is the only acceptable way to deliberately annoy your opponent.

## 1o. Play what you like

Play openings that appeal to you, openings you're comfortable with, openings you've chosen for your repertoire. Don't worry if your opponents know what you play. Don't venture into positions just to surprise your opponents, unless you're familiar with those types of positions yourself. The more you play, the better you'll get to know yourself as a player. Be exactly who you are, and go with the flow of your own personal playing style.

# 15. INSTRUCTIVE GAMES

## GAME 1: A BEGINNERS GAME

**WHITE: Sandy**
**BLACK: Matt**

|   | White | Black |
|---|-------|-------|
| 1 | e4    | e5    |
| 2 | Nf3   | Nc6   |
| 3 | d4    |       |

These moves represent an opening called the *Scotch Game*.

| 3 | ... | Bb4+ |
|---|-----|------|

More commonly played is 3) ...exd4.

| 4 | Nc3 |
|---|-----|

White pins her own knight. 4) c3 makes a better impression, chasing away the bishop.

| 4 | ... | d5 |
|---|-----|----|

| 5 | Bg5 | Nf6 |
|---|------|-----|

Now Black pins his own knight. Maybe 5) . . . f6 was a better move, chasing the bishop. Black seems to be copying White's moves, which is a bad idea. For instance, White could now play 6) dxe5, attacking the pinned knight on f6, though after 6) ...d4, Black gets some counterplay. In any case, a player who copies the opponent's moves just for the sake of copying moves is almost certain to lose the game.

| 6 | Bb5 | Bg4 |
|---|------|-----|

This position is symmetrical. One half of the board mirrors the other half. Notice that all four knights are pinned. Interesting, but someone really ought to take advantage of one of these pins by attacking the pinned piece a second time! This position looks like something you'd see at an art exhibit.

| 7 | Qd3 | dxe4 |
|---|------|------|

Forking White's queen and knight with a pawn.

| 8 | Qe2? | |
|---|-------|--|

Better was 8) Bxf6; Qxf6 9) Qxe4, etc. Or, 8) Bxf6; exd3 9) Bxd8; Rxd8, etc. Either way, White avoids losing material.

| 8 | ... | exf3 |
|---|------|------|
| 9 | gxf3 | Bf5 |

Black, being ahead in material, should probably simplify this position by trading pieces with 9) ...Bxc3+. Other strong looking options include 9) ...Qxd4 and 9) ...Qd5.

| 10 | 0-0-0 | |

Castling is okay, but White fails to take advantage of the pin. She could have played, for instance, 10) dxe5, winning a pawn and threatening the pinned knight on f6.

| 10 | ... | h6 |
| 11 | dxe5 | |

Notice the discovery on Black's queen by White's rook on d1.

| 11 | ... | Qe7 |
| 12 | Be3 | Nd7 |
| 13 | Nd5 | |

Threatens Black's queen and the undefended pawn on c7.

| 13 | ... | Qxe5 |
| 14 | Rg1 | |

14) Bxc6 wins a piece after 14) ...bxc6, 15) Nxb4.

| 14 | ... | Ba3 |

Much better was 14) ...Ba5.

| 15 | Nxc7+ | Kf8 |

If Black had played 15) . . . Qxc7, White would have played 16) Bf4+, a discovered check that wins material.

| 16 | Nxa8 | |

White falls for a mate in two! Better was 16) bxa3.

| 16 | ... | Qxb2+ |
| 17 | Kd2 | Bb4++ |

## GAME 2: A MASTER MINIATURE

**WHITE: Bobby Fischer (1972 World Champion)**
**BLACK: Reuben Fine (American Grandmaster)**
*New York, 1963*

| | White | Black |
|---|-------|-------|
| 1 | e4 | e5 |
| 2 | Nf3 | Nc6 |
| 3 | Bc4 | Bc5 |

This sequence of opening moves is called the Giuoco Piano. It's a solid opening in which both players develop quickly while fighting for control of those ever-important center squares.

| 4 | b4 | |

This move defines a variation of the Giuoco Piano known as the Evans Gambit. A **gambit** is a sacrifice (usually a pawn) early in the game, in exchange for a positional advantage, such as a lead in development or better attacking chances.

| 4 | ... | Bxb4 |
|---|-----|------|

The gambit can also be declined with a move like 4) ...Bb6, but in this case Black decides to accept the pawn. Now let's see what White has to show for the sacrificed pawn.

| 5 | c3 | Ba5 |
|---|----|-----|

Also playable is 5) ...Bc5, or 5) ...Be7

| 6 | d4 | |
|---|----|--|

White already has three positional advantages for the lost pawn: 1) several connected pawns forming a stronghold on the center squares, 2) mobility for his pieces, and 3) a half-open b-file, which could possibly be a good place for the a1 rook later on.

| 6 | ... | exd4 |
|---|-----|------|

White can't answer this move with 7) cxd4 because the c-pawn is pinned. But here White gives up two more pawns for what he hopes is a crushing attack against Black's uncastled king.

| 7 | 0-0 | dxc3 |
|---|-----|------|

At this point White is three pawns down, which is equal to having sacrificed a knight or a bishop. White had better start attacking in a hurry.

**8        Qb3**

Threatening 9) Bxf7+.

**8        ...        Qe7**
**9        Nxc3        Nf6?**

This allows White to open the e-file and launch a killer attack, though Black was in trouble already. Maybe better was 9) . . .Bxc3 (trading down when ahead), though after 10) Qxc3 attacking g7, White sill has the better winning chances.

**10        Nd5        Nxd5**

If Black had played 10) ...Qxe4, White might have answered 11) Bg5, threatening to win the knight on f6, or 11) Nxf6+.

**11        exd5        Ne5**

Not 11) ...Nd8, because it allows 12) Ba3, threatening the queen. Then, if Black tries to block the attack with 12) ...d6, White could play 13) Qb5+, forking Black's king and bishop.

**12        Nxe5        Qxe5**
**13        Bb2        Qg5**

Moving the queen out of harm's way, while still protecting the pawn on g7.

**14          h4**

Deflection.

| 14 | ... | Qxh4 |
| 15 | Bxg7 | Rg8 |
| 16 | Rfel+ | Kd8 |

or 16 . . . Bxel, 17) Rxel; Kd8 with the same result.

**17          Qg3!**

This stroke of genius compels Black's queen to either give itself up for capture, or abandon the h4-d8 diagonal, allowing mate. For instance, 17) ...Qxg3, then 18) Bf6++. A cute defensive try is 17) ...Qd4, but it loses anyway after, say, 18) Bf6+; Qxf6, 19) Qxg8++.

**17          ...          Black resigns**

## GAME 3: AN UPSET

**WHITE: Judee Shipman (Class A player)**
**BLACK: Kamran Shirazi (International Master)**
*New York, 1992*

|   | White | Black |
|---|-------|-------|
| 1 | e4 | e5 |
| 2 | Nf3 | Nf6 |

This opening is known as Petroff's Defense.

|   | White | Black |
|---|-------|-------|
| 3 | Nc3 | Bb4 |
| 4 | Bc4 | Nxe4 |

A common opening theme known as the fork trick. Black gives up the knight momentarily, but immediately wins it back by way of a pawn fork.

|   | White | Black |
|---|-------|-------|
| 5 | Nxe4 | d5 |
| 6 | c3 | |

Candidate moves here included 6) O-O, 6) a3, and 6) Bb5.

|   | White | Black |
|---|-------|-------|
| 6 | ... | dxc4 |

Black ignores White's 6th move, and seems to be losing material. A safer, simpler move was 6) ...Be7. But Mr. Shirazi is well known for playing odd moves that lead to mind-bending complications, and often confuses his opponents into blundering.

| 7  | cxb4 | 0-0 |
|----|------|-----|
| 8  | Qc2  | b5  |
| 9  | Neg5 |     |

Threatens 10) Qxh7++.

| 9  | ...  | f5  |
|----|------|-----|
| 10 | d3   | h6  |
| 11 | dxc4 | e4  |
| 12 | o-o  |     |

Avoiding typical Shirazi-style complications by giving back the knight and settling for a solid position with good development, a safe king, and an extra pawn. Now all I need is patience.

| 12 | ...   | exf3 |
|----|-------|------|
| 13 | Nxf3  | Bb7  |
| 14 | Qb3   | bxc4 |
| 15 | Qxc4+ | Bd5  |
| 16 | Qc3   | f4   |

Hindering the development of White's dark-squared bishop, so White plays a fianchetto.

| 17 | b3  | Nd7 |
|----|-----|-----|
| 18 | Bb2 | ... |

The bishop is quite happy on that long diagonal, and 19) Qxg7++ is threatened.

| 18 | | Rf6 |
|----|------|-----|
| 19 | Rad1 | Nb6 |
| 20 | Rd4 | |

Threatening 20) Rxf4, winning another pawn. If 20) ...Rxf4, then 21) Qxg7++.

| 20 | ... | Qd7 |
|----|-----|-----|

Develops the queen and defends g7, so the rook on f6 is free to defend the pawn on f4.

| 21 | Re1 | Re8 |
|----|-----|-----|

Losing the f-pawn, because White can make the queen leave its defense of g7, so the rook on f6 will be stuck there again, defending Qxg7 mate. But Black has nothing better at this point.

| 22 | Rxe8+ | Qxe8 |
|----|-------|------|
| 23 | Rxf4 | Bxf3 |

Hoping for 24) Qxf3, so Black can play 24) ...Qe1++!

| 24 | Rxf6 | Nd5 |
|----|------|-----|

This allows a combination. A better try was 23) ... gxf6.

| 25 | Re6 | |
|----|-----|---|

Threatens 25) Qxg7++ ...again.

| 25 | ... | Qf7 |
|----|-----|-----|

Necessary was 25) .. . Qd7.

| 26 | Re8+ | Kh7 |

If 26) ...Qxe8—you guessed it—27) Qxg7 mate.

| 27 | Qd3+ | Qg6 |

If 27) ...g6, 28) Rh8++!

| 28 | Rh8+ | |

Deflects the king away from the defense of his queen.

| 28 | ... | Kxh8 |
| 29 | Qxg6 | Black resigns. |

White still threatens Qxg7++. So, the following continuation would be forced:
29) ...Nf6 30) Bxf6; gxf6 31) Qxf6+; Kg8 (or Kh7) 32) Qxf3, and Black has no more pieces. White's queen and king will soon force checkmate.

# 16. PRACTICE PUZZLES

**Diagram D1**

White to play and mate in one move.

**Diagram D2**

Black to play and mate in one move.

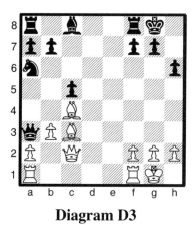

**Diagram D3**

White to play and mate in two moves.

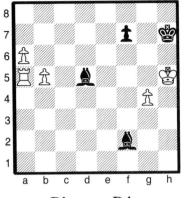

**Diagram D4**

Black to play and mate in two moves.

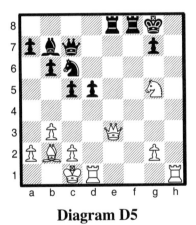

**Diagram D5**

White to play and mate in three moves.

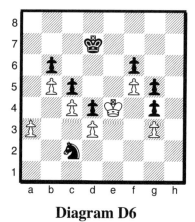

**Diagram D6**

Black to play and mate in three moves

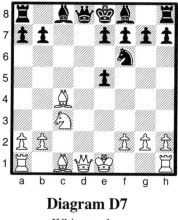

**Diagram D7**

White to play

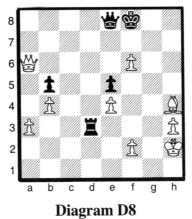

**Diagram D8**

Black to play

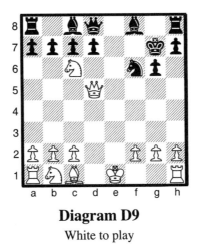

**Diagram D9**

White to play

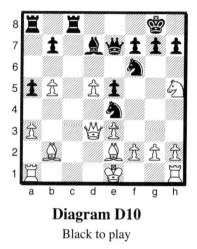

**Diagram D10**

Black to play

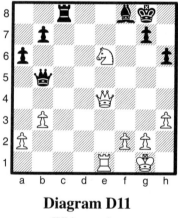

**Diagram D11**

White to play

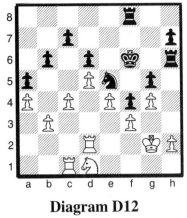

**Diagram D12**

Black to play

## ANSWER KEY

**D1** **1) Re8++**

**D2** **1) ...f2++**

**D3** **1) Qg6; any move by Black 2) Qxg7++**

**D4** **1) ..f6 2) almost any move by White; Bf7++**

Unless 2) g5, in which case 2) ...Bf3 is mate

**D5** **1) Rh8+; Kxh8 2) Qh3+; Kg8 3) Qh7++**

**D6** **1) ..Nxa3 2) Kd5; Nb1 3) Ke4; Nc3++**

**D7** **1) Bxf7+; Kxf7 2) Qxd8**

Tactic: Deflection

**D8** **1) ..Rxh3+ 2) Kxh3; Qe6+ 3) Qxe6, and Black has forced stalemate, drawing an otherwise lost position.**

Tactic: Desperado

**D9** **1)Bh6+; Kxh6 2) Qd2+; any 3) Nxd8**

Tactic: In-Between Move

**D10** **1)...Nxf2 2) Kxf2; Nxh5 3) Bxh5; Qh4+, followed by 4) ...Qxh5. Black wins a pawn and exposes White's king. Tactic: Fork**

**D11** **1)Ng5 (threatens Qh7++); hxg5 (or Qxg5) 2) Qe6+, followed by 3) Qxc8.**

Tactics: Clearance and Fork

**D12** **1) ...Rxh2+ 2) Kxh2; Nxf3+, followed by 3) ...Nxd2, and Black wins two pawns.**

Tactics: Deflection and Fork

# GLOSSARY OF CHESS TERMS

**Absolute Pin:** A situation in which a piece cannot move because it would be illegal (i.e. placing one's own king in check).

**Active:** The condition of a piece that has a lot of attack squares.

**Adjourn:** To stop a game temporarily, and resume it later on.

**Adjudicate:** To decide the result of an unfinished game based on the current position.

**Advance:** To move forward.

**Algebraic:** A modern type of chess notation where a square is named by its intersecting file and rank, respectively.

**Analyze:** To study a position or a game.

**Annotations:** Written comments pertaining to a recorded game.

**Attack:** To aim at a piece or a square, meaning that the piece or square can be reached in one move.

**Attack Square:** Any square a piece can reach in one move.

**Back Rank Mate:** A checkmate delivered by a rook or a queen on the 1st or 8th rank, often because a king is trapped behind its own pawn shield.

**Backward Pawn:** A weakness that occurs when a pawn cannot be defended by other pawns because those pawns are further advanced.

**Base:** The rear-most pawn of a pawn chain that is not protected by another pawn.

**Beginner:** Someone who is new to chess.

**Bishop:** A minor piece which moves diagonally; it is about equal in value to a knight.

**Bishops Of Opposite Colors:** A position where each player has a bishop, and one controls light squares, while the other controls dark squares.

**Black:** Refers to the player who doesn't move first and that player's pieces, regardless of what color the pieces actually are.

**Blitz:** A time control of five minutes or less per player.

**Blockade:** Usually refers to a piece that is placed right in front of an an isolated enemy pawn, in order to immobilize it.

**Blunder:** A very bad move.

**Book Move:** An opening move that falls within the boundaries of known opening theory.

**Building A Bridge:** An rook-and-pawn end game technique in which a player is able to promote by using his king and rook to prevent defensive checks from behind. Also known as the Lucena Position.

**Candidate Moves:** The moves being considered at any time during a game.

**Capture:** To remove an enemy piece from the board by moving your piece to a square that is occupied by that piece.

**Castle:** A single move in which the king travels two squares toward one of its rooks, then that rook moves to the other side of the king.

**Castling Into It (Slang):** Castling to the wrong place at the wrong time, thereby placing your king in the midst of an attack.

**Center:** The four squares in the middle of the chessboard—e4, e5, d4, and d5.

**Check:** A condition in which a king is threatened with immediate capture.

**Checkmate:** When a king is in check, and cannot get out of check.

**Chess Clock:** A double-faced clock that times the moves of both players.

**Closed File:** A file that is occupied by pawns of both colors.

**Combination:** A series of forcing moves that leads to some kind of positional improvement, such as material gain, mate, or successful defense.

**Compensation:** A positional advantage gained in return for lost material.

**Connected Pawns:** Pawns of the same color located on adjacent files.

**Control:** To attack a square so thoroughly that your opponent's pieces cannot safely go there.

**Coordination:** Cooperation among friendly pieces.

**Counterattack:** To attack while you are under attack.

**Counterplay:** Resourceful moves available within a position in which the opponent has the better game.

**Dark:** Refers to the darker squares, regardless of their actual color.

**Decoy:** A tactic that involves coaxing a piece towards a certain square (not to be confused with deflection).

**Defense:** The protection of a piece, or a square, from an enemy threat.

**Deflection:** A tactic that involves coaxing a piece away from a certain square (not to be confused with decoy).

**Demo Board:** A large chessboard with flat, oversized pieces, designed to hang on a wall for the purpose of demonstration to groups of players.

**Desperado:** A tactic that involves forcing your opponent to capture one or more of your pieces, but doing so damages your opponent's position in some way.

**Destination Square:** The square on which a piece lands when it moves.

**Development:** The act of giving your pieces better mobility than they had on their original squares.

**Diagonal:** A slanted line of same-color squares connected at their corners.

**Discovered Check:** A check by way of discovery.

**Discovery:** A tactic that involves attacking something with a particular piece, by moving another piece out of its way.

**Double Check:** A condition in which a king is checked by two enemy pieces at the same time. This can only happen by way of a discovery.
**Double Threat:** Two simultaneous threats against an opposing army.
**Doubled Pawns:** Two pawns of the same color located on the same file.
**Doubled Rooks:** Two rooks of the same color located on the same file.
**Draw:** A tied game.

**ELO:** The standard American chess tournament rating system, developed by Arpad Elo (pronounced EE-low) and sanctioned by the USCF.
**En Passant:** A pawn capture in which an enemy pawn may capture a pawn that moved two squares as if it had only moved one square.
**En Prise:** (pronounced on-PREE). See *HANG*.
**Endgame:** The last of the three stages of a chess game.
**Enemy Forces:** Your opponent's pieces.
**Entombed:** A condition in which a piece is blocked on all sides by its own men.
**Escape Square:** A safe square to which a piece can flee when under attack.
**Exchange: The:** A term used to describe the difference in value between a rook and a *minor piece*. Trading a knight or bishop for a rook or vice versa is known as winning (or losing) the exchange.
**Expanded Center:** The squares immediately surrounding the center squares.

**Fianchetto:** The development of a bishop onto a long diagonal, instead of toward the center. A bishop fianchettos to b2 or g2 for White; b7 or g7 for Black.
**FIDE:** The standard international chess rating system, pronounced FEE-day.
**File:** Any vertical column of squares on a chessboard, labeled *a* thru *h*.
**Fish:** Same as *patzer*, but playing for money.
**Fixed Pawns:** Two or more pawns preventing each other from moving.
**Flank Opening:** Opening in which a bishop develops by way of *fianchetto*.
**Flight Square:** Any square to which a piece can flee to safety.
**Fool's Mate:** Also known as the two-move checkmate. The game proceeds like this, with occasional, slight variations: 1) f4; e5 2) g4; Qh4++.
**Forcing Move:** A move which leaves your opponent no choice but to reply in a particular way. *Check* is a good example.
**Forfeit:** The loss of a game due to overstepping the time control, or through a penalty imposed by the referee.
**Fork:** A tactic by which a single piece makes two threats at once.
**Four-Move Mate:** See *Scholar's Mate*
**Friendly Forces:** The pieces in your own army.

**Gambit:** An opening *sacrifice*, usually a pawn, for a positional advantage.
**Guard:** To protect or defend a piece or square against a threat.
**Grandmaster:** The highest official chess title, other than World Champion. Achieved by a consistently high level of performance against other Grandmasters in International tournaments.

**Half Open File:** A file with only one player's pawn(s) on it.

**Hang:** To leave a piece where it can be captured for free, or for less than it is worth. A hanging piece is said to be *en prise*.

**Hole:** A square that is weakened because the pawns on the files adjacent to it are too far advanced to support that square. A hole is often the square immediately in front of a backward pawn.

**Illegal:** A move or position that is not possible, according to the rules of chess.

**Imbalance:** Positional inequality due to a difference in material, or a difference in the placement of forces between two players. Refers to a lack of symmetry.

**In-Between Move:** An advanced tactic by which a player inserts an unrelated forcing move into the midst of a combination.

**Initiative:** The ability to make threats.

**Interference:** A tactic that involves forcing your opponent's pieces to get in each other's way.

**International Master:** An official title granted to a player who performs at a consistently high level against other International Masters in international tournaments; one level below Grandmaster.

**Interpose:** To block a line of attack by placing a piece in between the piece that is threatened and the piece that is attacking it.

**Isolated Pawn:** A pawn with no friendly pawns on either adjacent file.

**J'Adoube:** A French term meaning "I adjust."

**Kamikaze:** see Desperado.

**Kibitz:** To comment on other people's games within earshot of the players.

**King:** The piece that must be trapped (checkmated) in order for a player to win.

**Kingside:** The side of the board on which the kings start the game.

**Knight:** A minor piece, shaped like a horse, about equal in value to a bishop.

**L-Shaped:** A visual description of the knight's trajectory.

**Landing Square:** The square on which a piece lands when it moves.

**Lawnmower:** See *Roll*.

**Legal:** Any move or position permitted, according to the official rules of chess:.

**Light:** Refers to the lighter-colored squares on a chessboard.

**Long Diagonal:** One of the two longest diagonals on the chessboard.

**Lucena Position:** See Building a Bridge.

**Luft:** German word for "air." A flight square for your king.

**Major Piece(s):** Rooks and queens.

**Master:** A player whose official rating is 2200 or more.

**Mate:** See Checkmate.

**Material:** The pieces, not including the king.

**Middle Game:** The second of the three stages of a chess game.

**Minor Piece(s):** Knights and bishops.

**Mobility:** Freedom of movement.
**Move:** Refers to either a single move played by one player, or a move pair—one move for each player. If a game lasted twenty moves, that means *each* player made twenty moves.

**Notation:** A system of recording moves.
**Novice:** Someone who plays chess on a purely recreational level.

**Occupy:** To physically be on a square. "A bishop occupies d3," means that a bishop is currently standing on the d3 square.
**Offense:** Any attack against an enemy piece, or square.
**Open File:** A file with no pawns on it.
**Opening:** The first of the three stages of a chess game.
**Opponent:** The player against whom you are competing.
**Opposition:** An endgame theme involving kings, in which the player who does not have to move has the upper hand.
**Overworked Piece:** A piece defending too many squares or pieces at once.

**Pass:** To give up one's turn, letting the opponent make two or more consecutive moves. This is never allowed in chess.
**Passed Pawn:** A pawn that cannot be stopped by enemy pawns.
**Patzer:** Slang term for a weak chess player.
**Pawn:** The least valued of the chess pieces.
**Pawn Chain:** Two or more pawns connected along a diagonal, so that each pawn, except for the base pawn, is defended by another pawn.
**Pawn Grabbing:** Impulsively capturing a pawn, while neglecting more immediate concerns in your position, such as king safety.
**Pawn Island:** A group of two or more pawns that stand on adjacent files.
**Pawn Majority:** More pawns on one side of the board than the opponent has on that same side. Usually known as a kingside or queenside pawn majority.
**Pawn Shield:** One or more connected pawns standing in front of a king, serving as a wall of protection from enemy forces.
**Pawn Storm:** Several neighboring pawns marching rapidly toward enemy territory, whether to attack the enemy king or to promote.
**Pawn Structure:** The way in which one's pawns are positioned in relation to each other at any time during a game.
**Perpetual Check:** An endlessly repeating series of checks.
**Piece:** May refer to any chess piece, as in "Set up your pieces and let's play!" Sometimes refers only to queens, rooks, knights and bishops, as in "Develop your pieces." Experienced players use the word to refer to a minor piece.
**Piece Count:** The total numerical value of all the pieces in a player's army.
**Pin:** A tactic by which a piece can't or shouldn't move, because doing so would expose another piece to attack.
**Play:** Dynamic possibilities in a position, like mobility or attacking chances.
**Poison Pawn:** A pawn that, if captured, would damage the position of the player who took it.

**Position:** The specific arrangement of the pieces at any point during a game.
**Positional:** The kind of chess game where players gradually improve their positions with subtle maneuvers, rather than playing for an all out atack.
**Promotion:** The changing of a pawn to a knight, bishop, rook, or queen, upon reaching the last rank.

**Queen:** The most powerful chess piece. It moves one or more squares in any direction.
**Queening a Pawn:** A common term for pawn promotion.
**Queening Square:** The square on which a pawn promotes.
**Queenside:** The side of the board on which the queens start the game—White's left or Black's right side.

**Race:** A position in which all that matters is who reaches a certain goal first; for example, two players racing their pawns toward queening squares.
**Rank:** A horizontal row of squares, labeled 1 thru 8.
**Rating:** An officially sanctioned numerical value that indicates a player's tournament performance level (which is an indication of playing strength), as compared to other players. The average chess rating in the United States is around 1550.
**Recapture:** To capture a piece in exchange for one that has just been captured.
**Relative Pin:** A situation in which a piece should not move because doing so would expose another piece to attack.
**Relative Value:** The worth of a piece as compared to other pieces.
**Removing the Guard:** A tactic involving the removal of a defending piece from its post, either by capturing it or forcing it to move.
**Resign:** To concede the game in a lost position, before checkmate has occurred.
**Retreat:** Generally speaking, to move a piece backward.
**Roll:** A sequence of alternating checks by two pieces of similar power, such as two rooks or two bishops, which forces the enemy king to an edge or a corner (a.k.a. *lawnmower technique*).
**Rook:** One of the major pieces, about equal in value to a knight and two pawns.
**Round Robin:** A tournament pairing system by which each player in the tournament plays at least one game against every other player.

**Sac:** See *Sacrifice*.
**Sacrifice:** To deliberately lose material in exchange for something more valuable.
**Scholar's Mate:** Also known as a four-move checkmate, it pertains to an attack against f7 or f2, using queen and bishop. A sample scholar's mate: 1) e4; e5 2) Nc3; Bc5 3) Bc4; Qh4 4) Nf3; Qxf2++.
**Scope:** See *Mobility*.
**Score Sheet:** A sheet of paper formatted for recording moves.
**Sharp:** Describes a move that is somewhat menacing.
**Simul:** A simultaneous exhibition with one person playing two or more opponents at the same time.

**Single Attack:** A direct attack on one piece by another piece.

**Single Threat:** One piece making one threat.

**Skewer:** A tactic by which two friendly pieces stand on the same rank, file, or diagonal, so that moving one exposes the other one to attack.

**Smothered Mate:** A checkmate in which a king is entombed by friendly forces.

**Space:** Any area of the chessboard, a square being the smallest unit.

**Spatial Advantage:** An advantage in space that occurs when a player's pieces control more squares than the opponent's pieces do, especially squares in the opponent's territory.

**Sportsmanship:** A code of conduct among chess players, generally pertaining to manners, etiquette, and respect for one's opponent.

**Stalemate:** A drawn game in which the player whose turn it is has no legal moves, but his king is not in check.

**Strategy:** A general plan of action for your pieces.

**Sudden Death:** A *time control* in which a player has to finish the whole game— as opposed to just a certain number of moves—in a set length of time.

**Swindle:** A tactic usually employed by a player who is losing. It involves making a move that, if answered correctly, damages your position even further. The move, however, entices an attractive looking reply, which is actually a mistake.

**Swiss System:** A tournament pairing system by which players are initially grouped and paired according to their ratings, then subsequently paired against players with the same cumulative score.

**Symmetry:** A position in which both players have the same pieces, and they are placed in such a way that one half of the board mirrors the other half.

**Tactics:** Tricks the pieces can do to gain an advantage.

**Take:** see *Capture*.

**Tempo:** A unit of time in chess, which manifests itself as the ability to make what amounts to an extra move.

**Territory:** The half of the board on which a player's army starts the game.

**Threat:** The ability to gain an advantage if allowed to do so.

**Time Control:** The amount of time allotted to each player for a certain number of moves, or for the entire game.

**Touch-Move Rule:** A rule by which a piece must be moved (or captured) if touched by the player whose turn it is to move.

**Tournament:** A chess competition in which each entrant plays several consecutive games against different opponents.

**Trade:** An even exchange of forces.

**Trajectory:** The squares over which a piece travels in a single move.

**Transpose:** To reach a known position by way of an unusual move sequence.

**Two-Move Mate:** See *Fool's Mate*.

**Under Defended:** A piece or a square that is not adequately defended.

**Underpromotion:** Promoting a pawn to something other than a queen.

**Upset:** A game in which a weaker player beats a stronger player (Most players agree that a rating difference of 400 points or more defines an upset).
**USCF:** United States Chess Federation.


**Vacating:** A tactic by which a piece moves off a square so that another piece can occupy that square.
**Variation:** Any reasonable sequence of moves available from a given position.


**Waiting Move:** A move that has no effect on the nature of a position, except to change whose move it is.
**Weakness:** A piece that is not well placed, or a square that is not adequately defended, and therefore susceptible to attack.
**White:** Refers to the player who goes first or that player's pieces.
**Windmill Attack:** A combination in which one piece is able to capture several enemy pieces via a series of discovered checks.


**Zugzwang:** A situation where any move you make will lose, but it's your move.

# ACKNOWLEDGEMENTS

*This book owes its existence to the encouragement, advice, talent, and support of the following very cool people:*

- *Walter Shipman, International Master and best dad ever.*

- *Bruce Pandolfini, master, writer, teacher, and most excellent friend.*

- *Frank Thornally, asskicking master and guardian angel.*

- *Tom Arnold, literary genius. (I don't know if he plays chess, and I don't care. How I Lost 5 Pounds in 6 Years is the best book I've ever read. I think I'm in love).*

- *My inquisitive students, who asked all the right questions. The answers, I hope, are here.*

Come visit us on the web!
www. cardozapub.com